"Jesus asked that we become disciples who make disciples (Matthew 28: 18-20). Most Christians would like to obey the Great Commission but lack confidence that they possess the ability and basic skills to succeed. In *Disciple-Makers Toolbox*, Jack Dannemiller addresses the need people have for basic disciple-making tools. Importantly, he addresses the need for loving conversation and dialogue with other people. I recommend this book to anyone who wishes to gain confidence that they can become a "disciple who makes disciples.""

— **Chris Scruggs,** *Retired pastor, spiritual friend, and author of* **Salt and Light: Everyday Discipleship and Crisis of Discipleship.**

"*Disciple Makers Toolbox* manages to bring together tried and true methodologies, metaphors, and helpful illustrations for communicating the good news of Jesus Christ in one concise resource. After having spent an hour or two with this accessible book, anybody could comfortably and winsomely sit across from somebody and communicate the gospel and God's desire for growing discipleship, regardless of where they were on their spiritual journey. It would hard to imagine a resource that communicated as much helpful, urgent information in so little space."

— **Rev. Dr. Ben Lee,** *President, In His Steps Foundation*

"*Disciple Makers Toolbox* is an amazing road map to evangelism and discipleship God's way! Jack has put together a broad collection of God honoring materials that will have an impact on the lives of so many! This material will really help the Christ follower mentor and disciple young and new Believers with well grounded Biblical follow-up materials. Truly AWESOME!"

— **David McDowell,** *Vice President Development and Global Initiatives, Athletes in Action*

"We found the *Disciple Makers Toolbox* very useful in giving us tools to help us fulfill the great commission, Jesus' command for all Christians. We highly recommend it's use by individuals who want to gain more confidence in how to answer questions that seekers or questioning believers have. It also would be an excellent study guide for Sunday schools and for churches in discipleship training and for Community group Bible studies. The tools in this manual will definitely give the Christian more confidence to approach people and help them learn of God's love for them as God desires that all people be saved. God wants them to have a personal relationship with Jesus because by following Jesus they will receive love, joy and peace like they have never known before and to know with certainty that their eternal destiny will be Heaven."

— **Wolf Kraft,** *Publisher and Author of German High School textbooks, and his wife,* **Rosie Kraft**

"We live in a day and age or truth is getting lost. Christians who battle the culture know that sometimes having a handy Toolbox for Discipleship would be amazing. Now finally one is available; the first it's kind! This *Disciple Makers Toolbox* by Jack Dannemiller is just that because at your fingertips you will have access to answers to tough questions, parenting tips on raising Christian kids and many tools for making disciples. This toolbox reminds me of the wisdom of a man who discipled me many years ago and it can disciple you today. If you're a parent, a grandparent, a kid in school, a Pastor, a teacher, a Chaplin or a young or mature Christian, this book is for you."

— **Andy Reid,** *Area Director, North Dallas Young Life*

"Jack Dannemiller is an expert discipler. He especially excels in teaching Christians to be confident in their faith and share it confidently with others. Through Jack's mastery of apologetics, he has given us the *Discipler-Makers Toolbox*: an indispensable and versatile resource. Not only does it function as a book to give away to your disciples, but as interactive material to use for one-on-one appointments, Bible studies, and small groups. Put this book in your own toolbox!"

— **Scott Sommer,** *missionary with Cru for 25 years, Theological Development Director, FBI - U.S. Secret Service, and hospice chaplain, M.Div from Ashland Theological Seminary, one of Jack's personal disciples for many years*

"The disciple making methods of Jesus are clear: disciples don't just appear. They are formed over time through practice and heart shaping interactions. Jack Dannemiller embodies this for me as a lifelong learner who understands the power of shaping souls through great questions and foundational spiritual practices. A craftsman masters his trade with lots of practice and expert use of the right tools. With great clarity fueled by an experienced passion Jack presents in this short book the essential tools to unlock a life of learning, joy in Christ, and faithful multiplication."

— **Keith Hileman,** *Pastor of Discipleship - Bay Presbyterian Church of Bay Village, Ohio*

"This is one of the most thorough and concise equipping resources I've come across in my 20+ years of ministry. This Instruction Manual will equip you to reach the lost. It equips a disciple-maker to ask probing questions to understand where the lost person is on their spiritual journey, all the way through to answering the most common objections to the Christian faith. Most importantly, it equips us with a clear understanding of what the gospel is, and how to communicate the gospel clearly to someone that wants to trust Jesus."

— **Carl Schweisthal**, *Director CRU City Columbus, Ohio*

"Jack has done an extraordinary job of stocking the Christian toolbox with accessible and compelling tools for the disciple of Jesus to engage their friends, family, and neighbors in the mission of Jesus Christ. This book will be a great resource to keep handy whether you're walking with a new believer through the essentials of the faith, or conversing with a curious doubter over the truth claims of the Bible, and the existence of God."

— **Doug Hummer**, *Associate Pastor Christian Discipleship, Sanibel Community Church, Sanibel, Florida*

"I was drawn to the excellent guide for experiencing the Bible included in this book. Jack has captured so many things in these brief pages that I can recommend it to those seeking a way to navigate the seemingly enormous task of exploring faith in the life of Jesus. We see so many examples in the world of sin, war, disease, and suffering - it is comforting to go back and study the basis for being saved by faith."

— **Martin Uhle**, *President and CEO, Community West Foundation, Westlake, Ohio*

DISCIPLE
MAKERS
TOOLBOX

JACK DANNEMILLER

DISCIPLE MAKERS TOOLBOX

INSTRUCTION MANUAL

Your Guide to Becoming a Disciple Maker

Living Dialog
MINISTRIES

Dedicated to the memory of my beloved wife, Jean Marie,
for all the encouragement she provided for nearly 60 years
to set aside precious time to create materials to equip
disciples and lead seekers to a personal relationship with
Jesus Christ, her Savior and mine.

Dedicated also to those who want to be fearless
and confident in sharing the good news of the Gospel
of Jesus Christ in this post-Christian era.

Disciple Makers Toolbox: Instruction Manual
© 2023 The Living Dialog Ministries (TLDM)
Published by The Living Dialog Ministries, Richmond, VA
www.livingdialog.org

The Living Dialog Ministries
PO Box 15125
Richmond, VA 23227

ISBN: 979-8-9863804-2-1

TLDM, Inc. is a tax-exempt organization under section 501(c) (3) of the Internal Revenue Code effective 2 December 2009. We do our work and fulfill our mission through the generous gifts of our friends around the world. Your tax-deductible gifts may be sent to TLDM — PO Box 15125 — Richmond, VA 23227

18 17 16 15 14 13   7 6 5 4 3 2 1

Printed in the United States of America

Cover Design: Marlene Asta

ACKNOWLEDGMENTS

This Instruction Manual, with its toolbox tools, would not have become a reality without the wise counsel, insightful contributions and life experiences of many associates, colleagues, family members, friends and Christian pastors who have labored in the 'Harvest' as disciples of Jesus Christ to present the "Good News" of the Gospel to seekers of the Truth of the God of the Bible about life, eternal life and one's eternal destiny. They are too numerous to mention individually by name for fear that some may be omitted due to my oversight. Their contributions to the content is what has made this manual so valuable as a resource to equip disciples for their mission to fulfill the "Great Commission." We owe them all a great debt of gratitude for their faithfulness.

The Living Dialog Ministries, TLDM, also is indebted to Katrina Salokar for the excellent graphics, formatting and editing of the manual by her design team at Paradise Creative Group including Marlene Asta, Frank Gutbrod, Garret Granitz, Ava St. Laurent Katrina Salokar and Heather Corbin. Credit for the eye-catching design cover belongs to Marlene Asta and for the suggestions to make it better by Brian Regrut which have further enhanced the contents of the instruction manual.

Finally, and most importantly, I want to acknowledge and thank my Lord and Savior Jesus Christ who has inspired this labor of love over the past two years. Jesus and the Holy Spirit have guided this project so that His Disciples can be better equipped to present the "Good News" of the Gospel, fulfill the Great Commission and bring Glory to God. Amen!

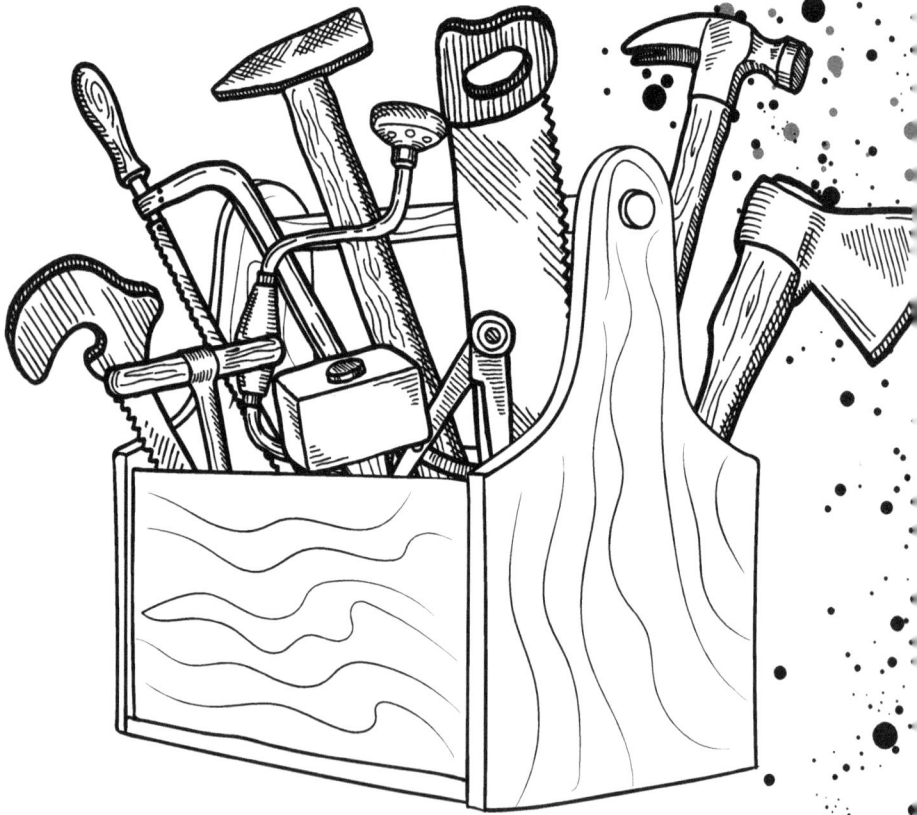

TABLE OF CONTENTS

FOREWORD
WRITTEN BY DR. G. LEE SOUTHARD

I have known Jack Dannemiller for 20 years. We have worked together in Sanibel Community Church on important leadership, financial, educational matters and discipling initiatives. For 10 years, we have been part of a special group of men who have been successful in their careers and also in their commitment and understanding of the Christian faith. If there ever was an "iron sharpens iron" group off men regarding the Christian faith, they are it and it has been our great privilege to co-labor with them in our fellowship groups.

Given Jack's track record as a successful servant leader CEO he knows that success in the completion of the mission in any organization requires tools and competent people to apply them. As a dedicated servant of Christ in the church and the public space he has seen firsthand the necessity for the tools of discipleship and the need to develop disciples capable of using them to make more disciples. In many cases the tools are there but lie unused.

When I think of a toolbox, I think of the old wooden box that carpenters and handymen dressed in overhauls took with them to every job. The box had everything needed to complete the job and the handy man had the experience to use them and be the Mister Fix-it.

Today's toolbox is more complicated and is usually a van or pick-up carrying many more sophisticated tools. The tools require a trained handyman from a trade school or college who is usually in a uniform. And has the experience to complete his tasks. He is today's Mister Fix-it.

Disciples of Jesus today are God's handymen. In God's eyes they are to live by the command of Jesus to make more disciples. Just like the tools in the toolbox of earlier handymen the modern day discipler needs the right tools to meet the challenges of today's "prove it to me" culture. Rarely can one witness to someone today and respond to their questions by just saying "because it's in the Bible". It may indeed be in the Bible but to a culture that increasingly is ignorant of the Bible that often won't fly. We still need the same tools from the old toolbox, but we need to supplement how we use them with the new tools of hard evidence of the faith that come from an Apologetics approach.

Research has shown that modern day disciples no longer possess the tools or the will to do the job. There are fewer of them every year primarily the result of lost youth to the church. As a result, people in need of fixing are increasing at a rate faster than disciple growth. When surveyed people who dropped out of the faith said they did not believe. Sixty-three percent said that a part of their youth was spent in the church. It is a battle, and we are losing. This is a national crisis, and it is only a matter of time before it will be beyond recovery. We are in need of a fix that only God can do but he needs capable handymen to help.

The church is the only institution with the mission and resources to fight this battle by training disciples with the tools to win. The church is in need of a major reexamination of its toolbox for making disciples. Give these disciples the tools to confidently fight the battle and effectively make new disciples. Such is the *Disciple Makers Toolbox*.

Jack Dannemiller has put together a modern disciple makers toolbox for the church to utilize in the creation of disciples capable of going into the world and making new disciples in today's culture. Parents also should take note of the tools listed to exercise their responsibility for the discipleship of their children. The church and parents fully committed to using these tools would be powerful combination in achieving the goal of Jesus' command to make new disciples including preparing existing disciples.

The toolbox identifies and answers important questions about the faith, includes important resources from noted spiritual leaders and suggestions on their use. It supplies everything one needs to know to be an effective disciple in making disciples.

As one very familiar with the battle it is my hope and prayer that the *Disciple Makers Toolbox* will become the instruction manual for every church, parent and people in leadership to engage in this battle by adopting the tools offered in this book. The tools are there. Now let's use them.

ABOUT DR. G. LEE SOUTHARD

A native Virginian and a graduate of the Virginia Military Institute, Lee also has an M.S. from George Washington University and PH.D. in chemistry from the University of North Carolina in Chapel Hill. His career consisted of 40 years in research and development of pharmaceuticals and biotechnology products including the positions of Board Chairman, CEO, and Chief Science Officer. He has over 40 publications and patents and contributed to the development of 10 marketed therapeutic products. He is the author of two popular new books, *To Know With CERTAINTY* and *The Battle We Must Not Lose*. In a dual career, he was an artillery, chemical and military intelligence officer that included two commands over his 26 years in the active and reserve US Army retiring as Colonel. Lee and his wife, Marilyn, of 51 years had four boys and six grandchildren. He is remarried to Nancy and they reside in Fort Myers, Florida.

There is no greater privilege
for Christians than to be partners
with Jesus in building His kingdom.

PREFACE
A letter to Disciple Makers

"As you are going in the world, make disciples."
[Mark 16:15]
'Jesus' Great Commission for all His Disciples'

Dear Disciple of Jesus,

Jesus wants each of his disciples to be equipped to fulfill the Great Commission recorded in Matthew 28:19 and Mark 16:15. The definition of 'equipped' is "supplied with the necessary items for a particular purpose." Items for effective discipleship include tools or 'talking pieces' or illustrations to assist in presenting the Gospel for the purpose of building God's kingdom and the salvation of human souls.

There is no greater privilege for Christians than to be recruited as a partner by Jesus for His purpose. There is also no greater joy in life than to see a person repent and accept Jesus as Savior and Lord. It is one of the most important ways you can store up treasures in heaven. Jesus said, "The Harvest is plentiful, but the workers are few." The objective of this book is to equip the 'workers' for the Harvest with a set of tools and resources to accomplish the work.

The Introduction, which follows this Preface, lays out a proven process for sharing the Gospel with confidence, boldness and success. A disciple of Jesus needs to become mature in the Christian faith by diligent study of God's Word, the Bible. It takes dedication and hard work to gain the necessary knowledge and understanding of the truths of the Scriptures and the evidence that affirms what Christians believe. What Christians believe, why they believe it and why it's important is known as Christian Apologetics. Two of the resources in the toolbox are abbreviated summaries of Christian Apologetics.

It does not take a seminary degree or a Bible college education to become a mature, equipped disciple. That preparation and education can be accomplished by attending discipleship classes, church Bible studies, Christian small group dialogs and personal time in the Word with Jesus. In addition, to commitment of the mind, what it takes is a heart willing to do what Jesus asks by making it a priority to prepare for the disciple makers' challenge to be a worker in the 'Harvest'.

One important additional thought to remember is that the Disciples spent three and a half years, 24/7, with Jesus being prepared to share the gospel and go make disciples of all nations. They witnessed all the miracles, heard his teaching and learned how to pray but still did not believe or understand who he was. However, it was after his resurrection appearances and his ascension into heaven and the gift of the Holy Spirit that they were transformed into fearless disciples. In fact, they were so committed that all but the Apostle John were martyred for their faith. They proclaimed Jesus crucified and resurrected as the only way to gain eternal life, peace with God and a home in Heaven.

As Jesus' disciples today, we can make the same commitment the Apostles made. We have all the evidence we need, including the records of the miracles, the exact words of Jesus' teachings, his verified resurrection, the Holy Spirit living in us and the necessary resources available to prepare us for the mission. If that weren't enough, we have the history of hundreds of millions of believers, the church, who became disciples. So it is with this confidence that today we, too, can be fearless and confident proclaimers of the Gospel!

Finally, remember what Jesus said, "If you love me, obey my Commandments." Sharing the Gospel is a privilege and labor of love for the Master.

Sincerely,
Jack Dannemiller
Chairman and CEO
Living Dialog Ministries

Jesus used illustrations, parables
and tools of dialogue to communicate
profound biblical truths.

INTRODUCTION

Welcome to your Disciple Makers Toolbox. Anyone can learn to use the tools in this Toolbox. Applying them will enhance your creativity and success in presenting the Gospel of Jesus Christ with boldness and confidence. Remember, Jesus used illustrations, parables and tools of dialogue, i.e., asking and answering searching questions like those in this Toolbox, to communicate profound Biblical truths. He discipled his Disciples and equipped them with the tools and Truths necessary for the success of building God's kingdom. As his disciple, we want you to be equipped for the Kingdom mission too. The Holy Spirit will be your teacher and guide on this journey. The paragraphs that follow will give you a preview of what it takes to be a Christian Disciple Maker.

When you look at workers involved in the construction trades, they all have tool boxes filled with better tools to accomplish their work. One only has to think about plumbers, electricians, bricklayers, roofers, and carpenters to picture the tools of their trade. However, whether in medicine, business, or construction trades, a learning experience is always required to use the tools properly. Surgeons, for example, spend ten years or more learning the techniques for arthroscopic surgery. Those who work in the trades are often required to undergo extensive apprenticeships and capability testing before becoming licensed professionals.

Disciples of Jesus Christ are no different than those who work in the professions, business, or construction trades. In order for Christians who follow Jesus to be effective in carrying out the great commission, they need to be trained and equipped with the knowledge of the Christian faith, the evidence for God, the truths and facts of the Bible, the historical records of Jesus's birth, teachings, miracles, death, resurrection and ascension into heaven from both the biblical and secular historical writings of that first century. This knowledge is often referred to as Christian Apologetics. Simply stated, apologetics covers what Christians believe, why they believe it and why it's important to know.

Obviously, becoming a mature disciple of Jesus, one who is capable of making other disciples and sharing his or her faith in the gospel message with confidence, takes time, dedication and extensive study to be prepared for the challenge of fulfilling the great commission, "go make disciples of all nations." Unfortunately, this is not an easy apprenticeship. It requires committing time to study the Old and New Testaments of the Bible, much prayer and seeking the guidance of the Holy Spirit. It requires acquiring skills in creating conversations using the technique of dialogue and active listening, which Jesus modeled as he asked and answered questions. Jesus' life offers us a perfect example of dedicated preparation and becoming equipped before he was ready to make disciples.

Another requirement of the apprenticeship will be to know and memorize a select number of Bible verses that logically present the plan of salvation. The good news is that only a handful of verses are necessary to commit to memory. The challenge will be to learn how to use those verses in a loving conversation with the another person.

If all of this work, study and preparation seems daunting, it is. Any important undertaking requires a commitment of time, effort and even sacrifice. Building God's kingdom, making followers of Jesus

Christ and sharing God's love are the principal reasons humankind was created in God's image. It brings God the Glory. There is no greater joy in life than seeing unbelievers come to faith and have their lives transformed by the power of God.

Leading someone to Jesus is a great way to store up treasures in heaven. The tools provided in this toolbox will equip and enable effective disciple-making. Remember, different tools are needed to address the many challenges encountered when 'working" to present the Gospel. The toolbox contains many tools for disciple-makers that can be used when facing all types of personalities, from atheists and agnostics to genuine seekers of God and truth. Building God's kingdom is the most exciting work project on the planet. You will now be able to go out and have the tools necessary to be a certified Master builder for God.

As humans we are created by God as
dualistic beings, meaning we are eternal
spirits having a physical experience.

THOUGHTS, IDEAS, & TRUTHS ABOUT ETERNITY
A PERSONAL MESSAGE FOR DISCIPLES OF JESUS FROM THE AUTHOR

These are some observations, thoughts, ideas, and truths that I have come to understand at the ripe old age of 84 from my 60+ year faith journey with Jesus. I want to share these 'Gems of Wisdom' with His disciples, who are equipped to become disciple-makers to fulfill the Great Commission. My objective is to pass along to the next generation a legacy of wisdom that will strengthen them on their Christian faith journey in what is becoming an increasingly hostile post-Christian era.

The prevalent ideologies of Evolution and secular humanism are being indoctrinated into our children and grandchildren through social media, television news, woke corporations, Hollywood, and now in the public education system in virtually every Western country. As disciples of Jesus, we need to confront this challenge to Christianity. It is a spiritual battle for the souls of everyone on the planet. We must put on the full armor of God daily, as it is a battle we cannot lose. The following are those "Gems" for your consideration.

As humans, we are created as dualistic beings. That means we are both physical and spiritual. We are both mortal and eternal. We are born physically alive and spiritually dormant. When we accept God's amazing gift of grace, i.e. eternal life, by entering into a personal relationship with Jesus Christ, we become spiritually alive as well. We then are able to see and experience things that were never possible before. The moment we accept

Christ as Savior and Lord, God's Spirit enters our very being and we begin to change from the inside out. Someday when our physical bodies die, our spirit/soul goes on to live forever.

Our spirit, the eternal you, ultimately has only one of two destinations at physical death. We will either spend eternity with God (Heaven or separated from Him, Hell). The choice of where we will spend eternity is ours. God is a gentleman. He does not force His love upon us. God certainly encourages us to make the right choice but gives us the free will to decide.

Unfortunately, too many choose the path that leads to destruction. God's gift of salvation is free. It's called Grace! Like all gifts, however, it needs to be accepted and opened to be received. I am always amazed that people reject God's offer of salvation and eternal life and choose to go to Hell. God would allow all to become sons and daughters, part of His family, but He does not force His will on anyone. The only way to the Father is through the Son, Jesus Christ *[John 14:6]*.

Life is a discovery and learning process. We marvel at God's incredible creation. We wonder why we are even part of the creation. We search for meaning and purpose in life. We wonder if God has a specific plan for our lives *[See Jeremiah 29:11]*. We can hardly comprehend that God wants each of us to be in a partnership with Him to build His kingdom. God reveals to us that we each have unique special gifts and talents to use in that effort. Again, the choice is ours. We can either use these gifts and talents selfishly for ourselves, or we can use them willingly for God's purposes. God's love for us is so great we can hardly comprehend it. It is an unfailing love that endures forever.

I know from personal experience that since I made Jesus Lord of every aspect of my life, He has opened doors of opportunity I could never have imagined. I have been blessed beyond my wildest dreams. Jesus did this for me and He can do it for you too. I am reminded every day of this profound truth, "Only one life, twill soon be past; only what's done for Christ will last." The things the world has to offer seem unimportant in light of eternity. Showing others the way to eternal life found only in Jesus gives life meaning, purpose and joy. When you become a mature disciple of Jesus and know the biblical truths and evidence for your faith, you will be able to proclaim the Gospel to everyone you encounter in life with confidence, boldness and courage.

Finally, I exhort you to diligently study the reference resources listed in this toolbox, learn the dialogue process and learn how to use the tools in the toolbox so that you will be equipped to fearlessly proclaim the Gospel as you are going in life. Remember, you never go alone! The Holy Spirit is your constant companion, teacher, counselor and spiritual guide, just as He was for the Apostles.

Now, may the Lord bless you and keep you. May Lord make his face shine upon you and grant you his peace now and forever.

Jack Dannemiller

---◆---

Life's profound questions; Why am I here?
What is my purpose? Does God exist?
Is there life beyond death?

---◆---

CHAPTER 1

CHRISTIAN DISCIPLE MAKERS TOOLBOX DIALOGUE

SHARING THE GOSPEL WITH CONFIDENCE, BOLDNESS AND SUCCESS

Dialogue is the ancient art of seeking truth by engaging others in searching for answers to the profound questions of life.

Why am I here? What is my purpose? Does God exist? Is there life beyond death? and many more.

Socrates became famous for developing the process of dialogue known today as the Socratic method. The greatest master of dialogue was Jesus. He modeled the process by asking and providing answers to the most important questions of life, faith, truth and eternity.

In dialogue the best practice is to be open-minded as you and the other person inquire, explore, discover and seek understanding of God's Word, the Bible. The goal being for the other party to get their questions answered, their curiosity satisfied and finally decide to follow Jesus. This chapter will prepare you to answer those questions and to share God's Truths with seekers and new believers in a simple and straight forward way. And, just like good sales people who are excited about their products or services, you will know how to present the Gospel message compassionately and effectively. So let's proceed to examine and dig into the art of dialogue.

First, know the features and benefits of your offer, in this case, the Gospel. Memorize the appropriate scriptures. [Resource: Pathway to Heaven "tool"- Pg 24]. Be prepared to share your personal testimony and be familiar with the evidence and facts for your faith from the resources in your toolbox.

Second, make sure you know how the Gospel creates value for the seeker or skeptic. In other words, why they should want to become a Christian [Resource: Why would anyone want to follow Jesus "tool"]. Remember, patience is a virtue when presenting the Gospel.

Third, proceed with confidence to identify the person's spiritual needs, i.e., they are a sinner, have broken God's laws and will face God's judgment and condemnation unless they repent, turn from their current ways, and accept Jesus as Savior *[Romans 3:23, 5:8 and 6:23]*.

Fourth, Pray for guidance from the Holy Spirit on how to engage with the other person and then begin the conversation and start the dialogue.

ALERT: If you get an "off-the-wall" question, don't panic! Don't get put on defense! Rather ask, "Why is that question important to you?" You just might uncover the real reason for their 'Unbelief.' These are the seven most likely unbeliefs to be raised during your conversation by both seekers and doubters alike. Should they arise, you must be able to provide answers spontaneously to build interest and state the evidence for your beliefs in the Christian faith. If you are unable to do so, you will likely very quickly lose the attention of the other party. These are the seven:

1. There is no proof that God of creation and the Bible exist.

2. How can you say that the Bible is God's inspired living Word and its content is Truth? There are lots of truths.

3. You can't be sure that Jesus is the only Savior and only way to God.

4. Jesus wasn't raised from the dead. Either his disciples stole his body and made up the story, or he wasn't dead to begin with.

5. Jesus is dead and he is not coming again.

6. There is no Heaven or Hell. When we die, that's the end.

7. I don't want to know a God that lets bad things happen to good people.

The following are some suggested opening questions:

- What spiritual community are you associated with?
- What church do you attend regularly?
- Who is Jesus to you? Or, who do you think Jesus is?
- How did you come to that understanding?
- Have you ever read who Jesus said he was?
- Would you be interested in knowing why Jesus is the most important person in all of human history? If YES, present the evidence and the facts. If NO, ask why not.

NOTE: These are just a few of the possible opening questions. See the 'Toolbox' for more questions for the dialogue as needed to continue the conversation. [More questions can be found in Answers to YOUR Greatest Questions, *page 194.]*

IMPORTANT QUESTION: Do you ever think about your mortality or what happens when your life ends? In the recent George Barna survey of Americans, when asked the question, "What do you think happens after you die?" 92% responded that they will go to Heaven. The Truth is that Heaven is not the default destination; Hell is. It is also a Biblical Truth that there is no purgatory, or reincarnation, or "It's just over."

- So, if your life ended tomorrow, what would you believe? Where do you think you would spend eternity? Why? Are you certain or do you just hope so?

- Affirm that there is life beyond the grave. Yes, you might wonder if this is true, but you can know for certain. It is the philosophical question of the ages. Would you like to know what the answer is? It comes directly from God.

    He [God] has also set eternity in the human heart; yet no one can fathom what God has done from beginning to end. [Ecclesiastes 3:11]

    For God so loved the world that he gave his one and only Son, that whoever believes in him shall not perish but have eternal life. [John 3:16]

- Why is that the truth? Because God, the Creator, is the source of Truth and is Holy and will not have sin or sinful people in His presence or in the Paradise of Heaven. God has given humans His rules and commandments for godly living to protect us. They are also designed to ensure that we don't harm others and that in all things we honor Him. Unfortunately, none of us are able to live up to the standards that God has set. We are all sinners and would be forever separated from God if not for the fact that the punishment for our sin was endured by Jesus on the Cross.

    For all have sinned and fallen short of the glory of God. [Romans 3:23]

- Therefore, the consequence of breaking God's laws is death! That is both physical death and spiritual death. Spiritual death is when the eternal you or your soul is banished from God's presence in Hell, forever. And Hell, whether you believe it or not, is **real**.

- Why the Cross? At the Cross, Jesus conquered death, Hell, and the grave and completed God's plan of forgiveness, redemption, and eternal life for all who trust in Jesus as Savior.

While we were yet sinners, Christ died for us. [Romans 5:8]

- **ASK**: Would you like to know what the Bible calls this sacrifice of Christ? If the answer is **NO, ASK** Why not? As it is one of the single most important events in human history, and proceed to the answer. If the answer is **YES**, say it's called God's Grace!

- **Grace is God offering something we don't deserve**. What is it? Jesus! Jesus, the Son of God, paid the penalty for our sin on the Cross. He paid the debt we could not because He was sinless and we are sinners. When you confess that you are a sinner, commit to repent of your sinful ways, ask Jesus to forgive you and become your Savior, you are 'born again' into the family of God, become a child of God and gain eternal life and the assurance of heaven. Further, you have essentially passed from death to eternal life in an instant. That is truly Amazing Grace!!

- At this point, go to the next step: **TRIAL CLOSE**.

- **TRIAL CLOSE**: At some point in the conversation you'll get to what is known as a 'trial close.' In other words, they might be ready to accept Jesus as Savior. So, ask them if they would like to pray to receive Him into their life and heart as Savior and Lord. If they hesitate or indicate they are not decided, it might be a good place to use the 'Bridge Illustration' [see pages 44-48] from the toolbox to show them that Jesus is the only way to bridge the gap between a sinful person and God. It is also a point at which you can ask if they understand the Bridge illustration that the Cross of Christ is the only way to peace with God and eternal life. That there is not a path of good works that earns salvation. Again you can ask if they have further questions.

- **Show them the bookmark** [see page 24 for example] -
"Pathway to Heaven and Eternal Life" and read the Bible verses out loud. Their reply might be no or that they need more time to think about making the decision. You should affirm that it is a serious commitment not to be taken lightly. You should ask them when they believe they will decide. Offer to follow up by phone or in person. Again, you should affirm that it is the most important decision in life and agree that it needs to be considered seriously. It is the one choice that determines their eternal destiny and will reveal God's purpose for their life.

- Be sure to thank them for listening. Tell them you'll be praying for them and looking forward to the next conversation. Offer them a copy of the *Answers to Life's Basic Questions* booklet and/or *The Light of the World* booklet to read while they are deciding.

- HOWEVER, if the answer is **YES**, CLOSE the conversation with the 'sinners prayer" from the toolbox or the bookmark and recite the Scripture from *Romans 10:9 and 10* and ask them if that is the decision they want to make. Again, if the answer is **YES**, lead them in a prayer of repentance and acceptance of Jesus as their Savior.

If you declare with your mouth, "Jesus is Lord," and believe in your heart that God raised him from the dead, you will be saved. For it is with your heart that you believe and are justified, and it is with your mouth that you profess your faith and are saved. [Romans 10:9,10]

WARNING: *It is seldom that in one conversation an individual will be ready to make life's most important decision. It certainly can and does happen, but don't lose heart and don't get discouraged if they need more time.*

FINALLY, You will encounter times when you try to begin a conversation with someone about faith or God and Jesus and they immediately turn it off or redirect the conversation and change the subject. They could say they don't believe in God or the Bible or that there is life after death or that Hell is a real place or whatever. All you can do then is to politely and graciously end the conversation. Say you will be praying for them. Offer them the Answers booklet. Later pray that God will open their heart to receive the gospel.

REMEMBER, we are the messengers and that the Holy Spirit does the convicting and saving and that God's Word never returns empty.

Pathway to Heaven & Eternal Life

"For all have sinned and broken God's Laws." *(Romans 3:23)*

"But God demonstrates His own love for us in this: while we were still sinners, Christ died for us." *(Romans 5:8)*

"The wages of sin is death." All die! [both physical and spiritual death] *(Romans 6:23)*

"Unless someone is born again, he cannot see the kingdom of God." *(John 3:3)*

"God so loved the world that He gave His only begotten son, Jesus, that whoever believes in him will not perish but have eternal life. *(John 3:16)*

Jesus said, " I am the way, the truth and the Life. No one comes to the Father except through me." *(John 14:6)*

"If you confess with your mouth that Jesus Christ is Lord, and believe in Your heart that God has raised him from the dead you will be Saved." *(Romans 10:9&10)*

"I stand at the door and knock. If anyone hears my voice and opens the door,(Your Heart) I will come in." *(Revelation 3:20)*

Salvation is by God's Grace alone, through Faith alone,in Christ alone! There is no other name by which one can be saved or gain eternal Life!

Source: Disciples Makers Toolbox Bookmark [Front]

A *Sinners* Prayer of *Confession*

Lord Jesus, I confess I am a sinner
In need of a savior. I admit I have
Broken your commandments.
Please forgive me.

I invite you now into my heart as my
Savior and Lord of my life.

I commit to repent from my sinful
ways and thoughts and follow you
all the days of my life.

I believe in my heart that you died
on the Cross to pay the penalty
for my sins.

I believe that you are the resurrected
Messiah, Son of God, and are now
seated at God's right hand hearing
and accepting me as a child of God!

I thank you Jesus for your Amazing
Grace that saved a sinner like me!

Next Steps in Your *Faith Journey*

First, share this exciting news with
family, Friends and everyone you
encounter. Spread the Good News
of Jesus Christ with those you meet.

Next, begin reading your Bible daily.
Start with the Gospel of John to get
a first hand account of the life of
Jesus. Read a daily Devotional.

Then attend a Christ centered, Bible
teaching church, join a Bible study
and use you talents to serve God!

Living Dialog MINISTRIES

www.livingdialog.org

Source: Disciples Makers Toolbox Bookmark [Back]

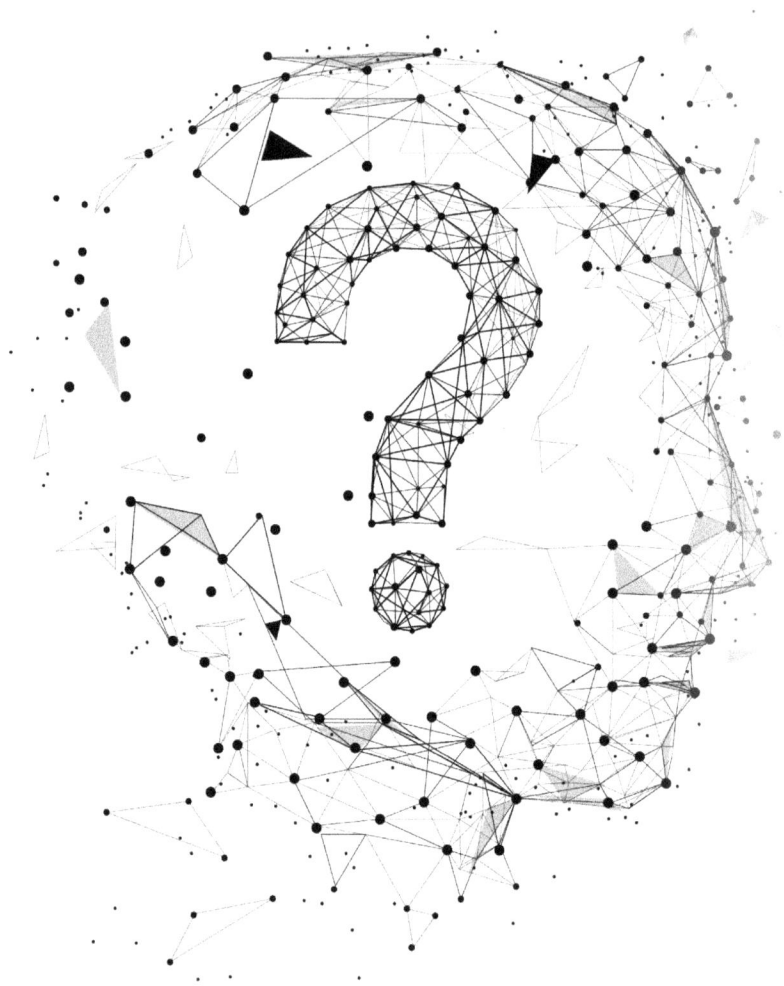

CHAPTER 2

MORE DISCERNING QUESTIONS FOR DIALOGUE

The first principle of Christian dialogue is to ask your questions with love and grace. It is true that people don't care how much you know until they know how much you care. These questions are designed to 'draw out' the other person's beliefs and perspectives and engage them in a discussion that leads to sharing Biblical truths and the Gospel. The questions that follow are supplemental to the opening questions in the Disciple Makers Toolbox Dialogue found in the preceding chapter. They offer some alternative ways to direct the conversation. Remember, it is essential to be an attentive listener.

Here are the questions:

- That's curious. Where did you get that idea? Are there facts that support that view?
- How do you know those facts are true? What is the evidence?
- What assumptions underlie that thought?
- What makes you think that's a good idea?
- Can you tell me some more about that?
- Can you give me an example that supports what you just said?
- I am not sure I understand what you said. Would you please repeat it?
- That's interesting. Would you tell me some more about it?
- If what you believe was not true, would you want to know?

Each encounter presents different challenges, so disciples need to have flexibility in how they direct the dialogue. When the Holy Spirit leads a discussion to spiritual matters you can ask, "So how are you with Jesus?" This is a slight rephrasing of the opening question, "Who is Jesus to you?"

This question can open up a special opportunity to share the gospel message, your story, and the love of God with someone who is genuinely seeking answers to some of life's most searching questions.

At some point in the conversation, a good question would be, "Would you like to know Him?" They may even be ready to pray to invite Jesus into their life as Lord and Savior. All that's left to do then is to lead them in prayer to accept Jesus and begin their faith journey. Then you can talk about the next steps in their new Christian life, such as reading the Bible, locating a good Gospel preaching, Christ-focused church and getting connected with a small group Bible study. You could even recommend the website godlife.com, where they can find a resource titled, *30 Days Next Steps* by John Beckett.

On the other hand, there still may be more questions that need to be discussed before a decision for Christ can be made. If time runs out, it would be good to provide them a copy of the *Answers to Life's Basic Questions* booklet and/or *The Light of the World* booklet, then arrange for a follow-up conversation.

CHAPTER 3

SEEKERS AND SKEPTICS FAQ'S BIBLICAL ANSWERS

QUESTIONS ABOUT GOD, JESUS, THE BIBLE AND CHRISTIANITY THAT YOU NEED TO BE ABLE TO ANSWER.

These questions are ones Disciple Makers will definitely encounter and ones which must be answered with both evidence and reason. The Apostle Paul is frequently quoted as "Reasoning" with those to whom he is presenting the Gospel and providing evidence of Jesus resurrection and being the promised Messiah and the Son of God [Acts 17:2, 18:9].

On the following pages are selected questions and abbreviated answers from Jack Dannemiller's *Answers to YOUR Greatest Questions* and Dr. G. Lee Southard's *To Know with Certainty*. We strongly recommend acquiring and reading each of these books so you can see more complete answers to these and scores of other questions asked by unbelievers and believers alike. The pages where those Qs and As appear in the respective books are noted by "A" for *Answers to YOUR Greatest Questions* and "T" for *To Know with Certainty*.

Of course, you can also search for and find the answers in a good reference Bible like, *The Life Application Bible*. We have tried to make it easier for you to find the answers with the noted pages in the two books. Remember, becoming a confident and effective Disciple Maker requires study and preparation but it is worth the effort as the rewards are eternal.

* **How do I know that God exists?** Evidence. Intelligent design of the universe and all nature, i.e., DNA, and the intricate laws that govern the sciences. *T p.1, A p.11*

* **How do I know the Bible is God's Word?** Prophecy. God knows the future as He exists outside of time and space. The Bible is a miracle as it was written over a period of 1,500 years by 40 authors and is in complete harmony with no contradictions. *T pp.21-24, A pp.125&153*

* **Was Jesus a real historical person?** Evidence. The biblical and secular records, Josephus' and Tacitus' historical Chronicles of the period, confirm Jesus as an authentic historical person. *T p.7*

* **How can I know that Jesus was the promised Messiah?** Prophecy. Jesus fulfilled over 100 prophetic pronouncements, many dating back 1,000 years before his birth, of his being the promised Messiah. *T p.9, A p.72*

* **Did Jesus really come back from the dead?** Evidence. Jesus was seen by the 11 disciples at least three times and by over 500 other witnesses during his 40 days on the earth after his resurrection prior to his ascension into heaven which was witnessed also by many. Jesus resurrection became the foundation of the Christian faith and the good news of the gospel. *T p.15, A p.74*

* **Don't all religions offer a path to God & Heaven?** No. Jesus stated himself that he is the only way to eternal life, peace with God and heaven *[John 14:6]*. The founders

of all the other world religions are dead. They offered no hope for eternal life. *A p.155*

● **Is Christianity exclusively claiming Jesus is the only way to Heaven and eternal life?** Yes. The Bible confirms it in many verses. *A p.71, [John 3:16, 1 John 5:11-12]*

● **How could a loving God condemn anyone to Hell?** God does not. People reject his gracious offer of salvation in Jesus and choose to go there. A loving God wants all to have a relationship with him, but each person has a free will to decide. God honors the choices that they make. *A p.20*

● **Why would anyone want to follow Jesus?** Benefits. Jesus alone offers meaning and purpose for life, answered prayers, eternal life and the gifts of the spirit; joy, love, peace, patience, kindness, goodness, faithfulness and so much more. *A p.78*

● **Isn't the Bible full of contradictions?** No. There are different descriptions of a few events just like witnesses' observations of a crime or accident but no contradictions. So, when accounts of events are taken as a composite a more complete description is provided. *T p.35, A p.130*

● **Why should I believe in creation rather than Evolution?** Evidence. Fossil record supports and confirms creation. There has never been a single piece of transitional evidence to demonstrate one species becoming another, i.e., Evolution. There are mutations and variations within species, but dogs are still dogs and horses are still horses. Science has now confirmed that there are at least 50 variables that must be perfectly in place for there to be any lifeforms whatsoever on planet earth. This is known as the Anthropic Principle. The probability of these factors existing from Evolution is zero. In fact, Evolution is a religion, no God, masquerading as a science, no evidence. *T pp. 81-91, A p.43*

These 11 Frequently Asked Questions above were taken from surveys of church pastors, leaders of Christian ministries like FCA, Young life, Athletes-in-Action, CRU (Campus Crusade) and chaplains of professional and scholastic sports teams regarding Life and Christian faith issues.

Those surveys also pointed to several additional profound FAQs. The most significant one was, How does one become a Christian and gain eternal life? The second logical follow-up question was, What are the Next Steps in the Christian life journey?

Answers to both of these questions and others can be found in our booklet, *Answers to Life's Greatest Questions*. For your Quick reference and convenience we have provided below the answers to the two profound FAQs mentioned above. We would encourage you to obtain a copy of the Answers booklet at our LivingDialog. org website so that you can be familiar with more of the questions from the surveys.

QUESTION: How does one become a Christian?

ANSWER: There is only one way to become a Christian. You must sincerely invite Jesus into your life to be Lord and Savior, and allow yourself to be 'born anew'. When you do, you find new life in Jesus Christ and become a child of God. Through this transformation you can find Peace, Joy and Courage to live a victorious Christian life. The choice is yours. God has given every person the free will to accept or reject his offer of grace. It is not something we earn but is freely given. Jesus already paid for it through His death on the Cross.

For it is by grace you have been saved, through faith—and this is not from yourselves, it is the gift of God. [Ephesians 2:8]

If you declare with your mouth, "Jesus is Lord," and believe in your heart that God raised him from the dead, you will be saved. For it is with your heart that you believe and are justified, and it is with your mouth that you profess your faith and are saved. [Romans 10:9-10]

QUESTION: What are the Next Steps in the Christian life Journey?

ANSWER: Every journey begins with a single step. Yours began when you admitted to God you were a sinner in need of a savior and asked for his forgiveness. Repenting of your old ways was the second step and inviting Jesus Christ into your life was the third. With those steps taken, you are well on your way to your new life in Christ.

As with any journey, you will encounter obstacles along the way. After all, you have a lifetime of experiences choices and regrets, accomplishments and defeats and probably even shame. You have also been subjected to the influence of others and by friends on social media. Some of your acquaintances may not want you to enjoy the fullness of your new life that comes from your relationship with Jesus.

That is why you need to get to know God and his son Jesus. The best way to get to know him is by reading his word, the Bible. Start with the book of John, which offers a first-hand account of the life of Jesus.

Next get connected with a Christ-centered, Bible-teaching church that will provide help with your spiritual growth. To encourage and help you along this new journey, feel free to visit our website, livingdialog.org. There you'll find more books and study guides to help you grow in your relationship with Christ and become more like Jesus everyday.

Over time you will come to fully understand What Christians believe, Why they believe it, Why it's important and Why it's true. Then you will be equipped to share Jesus with confidence with everyone you meet along your life journey.

"For God so loved the world that he gave his one and only Son, that whoever believes in him shall not perish but have eternal life."

[John 3:16]

A final thought for this chapter. When you start this journey with Jesus, it will be the adventure of your lifetime. You will learn not to fear the uncertainties of life because Jesus has promised to never leave you or forsake you. You will know with certainty that you have eternal life. You can stand on His promises. You will have forgiveness of your sins and peace with God. You will never again be intimidated or distressed by death. Jesus will fulfill your heart's desires with abundant blessings.

In Jesus you will have everything you need in life; joy, hope, happiness, wisdom, God's grace and love that endure forever. You will be a child of God and a joint heir with Jesus. It does not get any better than this!

---◆---

This journey with Jesus will be the
adventure of your lifetime. You will be
equipped to share Jesus with confidence!

---◆---

fields. ⁹ Those who went ahead and those who followed shouted,

"Hosanna!"

"Blessed is he who comes in the name of the Lord!"

¹⁰ "Blessed is the coming kingdom of our father David!"

"Hosanna in the highest heaven!"

¹¹ Jesus entered Jerusalem and went into the temple courts. He looked around at everything, but since it was already late, he went out to Bethany with the Twelve.

Jesus Curses a Fig Tree and Clears the Temple Courts

¹² The next day as they were leaving Bethany, Jesus was hungry. ¹³ Seeing in the distance a fig tree in leaf, he went to find out if it had any fruit. When he reached it, he found nothing but leaves, because it was not the season for figs. ¹⁴ Then he said to the tree, "May no one ever eat fruit from you again." And his disciples heard him say it.

¹⁵ On reaching Jerusalem, Jesus entered the temple courts and began driving out those who were buying and selling there. He overturned the tables of the money changers and the benches of those selling doves, ¹⁶ and would not allow anyone to carry merchandise through the temple courts. ¹⁷ And as he taught them, he said, "Is it not written: 'My house will be called a house of prayer for all nations'? But you have made it 'a den of robbers.'"

¹⁸ The chief priests and the teachers of the

law heard this and began looking for a way to kill him, for they feared him, because the whole crowd was amazed at his teaching.

¹⁹ When evening came, Jesus and his disciples went out of the city.

²⁰ In the morning, as they went along, they saw the fig tree withered from the roots. ²¹ Peter remembered and said to Jesus, "Rabbi, look! The fig tree you cursed has withered!"

²² **"Have FAITH in God," Jesus answered.**
[Mark 11:22]

²³ "Truly I tell you, if anyone says to this mountain, 'Go, throw yourself into the sea,' and does not doubt in their heart but believes that what they say will happen, it will be done for them. ²⁴ Therefore I tell you, whatever you ask for in prayer, believe that you have received it, and it will be yours. ²⁵ And when you stand praying, if you hold anything against anyone, forgive them, so that your Father in heaven may forgive you your sins." ²⁶ The Authority of Jesus Questioned

²⁷ They arrived again in Jerusalem, and while Jesus was walking in the temple courts, the chief priests, the teachers of the law and the elders came to him. ²⁸ "By what authority are you doing these things?" they asked. "And who gave you authority to do this?"

²⁹ Jesus replied, "I will ask you one question. Answer me, and I will tell you by

what authority I am doing these things. ³⁰ John's baptism—was it from heaven, or of human origin? Tell me!"

³¹ They discussed it among themselves and said, "If we say, 'From heaven,' he will ask, 'Why didn't you believe him?' ³² But if we say, 'Of human origin' …" (They feared the people, for everyone held that John really was a prophet.)

³³ So they answered Jesus, "We don't know."

Jesus said, "Neither will I tell you by what authority I am doing these things."

12 Jesus then began to speak to them in parables: "A man planted a vineyard. He put a wall around it, dug a pit for the winepress and built a watchtower. Then he rented the vineyard to some farmers and moved to another place. ² At harvest time he sent a servant to the tenants to collect from them some of the fruit of the vineyard. ³ But they seized him, beat him and sent him away empty-handed. ⁴ Then he sent another servant to them; they struck this man on the head and treated him shamefully. ⁵ He sent still another, and that one they killed. He sent many others; some of them they beat, others they killed.

⁶ "He had one left to send, a son, whom he loved. He sent him last of all, saying, 'They will respect my son.'

⁷ "But the tenants said to one another, 'This is the heir. Come, let's kill him, and the inheritance will be ours.' ⁸ So they took him and killed him, and threw him out of the vineyard.

CHAPTER 4
THE BLIND FAITH ISSUE

When trying to share the Christian faith with seekers or unbelievers, you can frequently run into the statement that Christianity is a blind faith because you can't see God. They often come to the issue with the perspective that reality is only what can be seen, not what is unseen. Not a true statement!

The fact of the matter is that everyone lives by Faith every day, whether they admit it or not.

Some examples are:

- **Highway Lane Dividing Lines** – Drivers have Faith that others will stay on their side of the road and obey DOT laws.

- **Elevators** – People who ride elevators have Faith that the intelligent designer, Otis, has assured them they are safe.

- **Airplanes** – Passengers have Faith in the intelligent design of Boeing that the plane will take off, fly and land safely. In fact, passengers have Faith in the principles of flight, as evidenced by the Wright brothers' success.

Further, every person believes in the unseen based on the evidence that is seen.

Some examples are:

- **Wind** – We see the evidence in the trees, in the clouds, on the water, and can feel the evidence on our skin, and we all know about wind chill. However, no one has ever seen wind.

- **Tides** – When you go to the ocean you can see the effect of tides moving in and out but not the force that causes them.

- **Gravity** – You cannot see the law of gravity, but you experience it every day. As Newton observed, apples fall from trees, and when we fall we go down, not up.

- **Earth's Rotation** – We cannot feel Earth's rotation at more than 1,000 mph. However, we observe sunrises and sunsets and 24-hour days.

- **Earth's Magnetic Shield** – It deflects Space junk from bombarding the earth and destroying life!

- **Light**- We observe the sun's light but cannot see it traveling at 186,282 miles per second. We believe it because it is true.

- **Dinosaurs**- We have never seen a live dinosaur but we have seen the fossil evidence so we believe that they existed.

- **Universe Expansion**- We cannot see or feel our universe expanding but we believe it is because the galaxies are moving further apart based on evidence on the Webb and Hubble telescopes. It is called the cosmological constant which is now included in Einstein's Theory of Relativity.

"*God alone stretches out the heavens*"
Job 9:8

$$E=MC^2$$

"*The heavens declare the glory of God; the skies proclaim the work of his hands.*"
Psalm 19:1

CHAPTER 5

GOD'S RULES -THE HUMAN FAMILY ANALOGY

Loving parents establish rules of behavior for raising their children just as a loving God provided the 10 Commandments as rules for human behavior. God desires that His children have a loving relationship with him and know him intimately and personally. That is why those who come to Him by Faith are referred to as the family or children of God.

So why rules? Think about it this way. Parents love their kids and want a loving relationship with them. Parents, just like God, want their children to become happy, honest, morally right, be of honorable character, trustworthy, loving, kind and thoughtful and much more. Parents guide children so that they will discover the meaning and purpose of their lives and live it in a way that honors God. Why? So that they can enjoy God's presence, experience His peace, acquire wisdom and understanding, and gain eternal life. That is how they can be with their loving family, Christian friends, and parents for all eternity. God and parents, both out of love, have lots of good reasons for rules. Also, a moral, just and safe society requires rules of behavior.

*Note: See the more comprehensive list of **what parents want for their children** from the Discipleship Resources and References [See Page 68].*

The process of raising godly children is always a challenge. When they break the rules, consequences must follow. It's often called tough love. Without discipline and standards for acceptable behavior the outcome is never good for the child or the parents.

REMEMBER, parents still love their children like God loves his children even when they are disobedient and break the rules. Forgiveness is offered when children's behavior changes, i.e., they repent and seek forgiveness and rules are honored to restore a loving, obedient relationship.

Now back to God and His rules as our Heavenly Father. What does God say in the Bible about the human condition and its behavior?

- All have sinned *[Romans 3:23]*
- The wages of sin is death *[Romans 6:23]*
- While we were still sinners, Christ died for us *[Romans 5:8]*

But what does God want for those created in his image? He wants them to enter into a personal relationship with Him through his son Jesus Christ. To be conformed into the image of Jesus means to develop His character qualities, including the following:

- If you declare with your mouth, "Jesus is Lord," and believe in your heart that God has raised Him from the dead, you will be saved. For it is with your heart that you believe and are justified, and with your mouth that you profess your faith and are saved. *[Romans 10:9, 10]*

- Salvation is by God's Grace alone, through Faith alone, in Christ alone. Jesus is the only way to have a relationship with God, experience His peace and receive eternal life. *[John 14:6]*

To be conformed into the image of Jesus means to develop His same character qualities, including the following:

- Love and Compassion
- Meekness - 'Strength Under Control'
- Servant's Heart
- Faithfulness
- Obedience
- Endurance
- Loyalty
- Righteous Indignation
- Generosity
- Joyfulness
- Sincerity

To become more like Jesus, God wants us to have a continual consciousness of Him through prayer and meditation.

God also wants us to become mature disciples of Jesus, being fully equipped to engage in the cause of the Great Commission of sharing the gospel.

God's expectations for all those who put their trust in Jesus, his children in the family of God, are motivated by God's sacrificial, unconditional love that endures forever.

*NOTE: For more detail on **what God wants for his children**, check the Discipleship Resources and References - pg 66.*

CHAPTER 6
DISCIPLESHIP EQUIPPING TOOLS

CHRISTIANITY VERSUS ALL OTHER RELIGIONS

What makes Christianity unique when compared to the other world religions? This is a frequent topic of conversation among Christians, those who are of different religions and those seeking answers to life's basic questions about God and eternity. Many believe that all religions offer a path to God and being created in the 'image of God' makes everyone a 'child of God.' In this section we're going to explain why these beliefs are not true.

The seven paragraphs that follow provide a robust and comprehensive perspective on the subject. We believe these paragraphs bring consistent clarity to this topic.

ANSWERS TO THE QUESTION:
What Makes Christianity Unique Compared to Other World Religions?

1. The simple answer is, Jesus! Why? Because He alone saves *[John 14:6]*. Only Christianity offers absolute assurance of eternal life as it is a gift of God's grace for all who by faith trust in Jesus as Savior and Lord *[Ephesians 2:8]*. Christianity is about Jesus, the Cross (forgiveness of sins), and his Resurrection, and Ascension, and his second coming. This is the Gospel and the foundation upon which Christianity is based. That is the Good News! Christianity is unique among all other religions in that it is based not on what a person does to gain favor with God, but what God has

done to restore the broken relationship between man and God. It is known as God's Amazing Grace!

2. Jesus is the answer because salvation is by God's Grace alone, through Faith alone, in Jesus Christ alone. Therefore, there is no condemnation for those who are in Christ Jesus *[Romans 8:1]*. Jesus is the resurrected Messiah and Savior and the only advocate and intercessor between man and God. In contrast, the founders of all other religions are dead. They have offered some sound platitudes for living a moral life but no hope for eternity based on solid evidence. They are religions of good works and self-sacrifice to gain a pardon for the worshiper's sins. Christianity is unique in that only by faith in Jesus are sins forgiven, is Peace with God possible and eternal life assured. He is coming back one day as King of Kings and Lord of Lords to be the righteous ruler over all the earth.

3. The person of Jesus Christ and the Holy Bible differentiates Christianity. The Cross of Christ forever bridged the gap between sinners and a Holy God. The Bible, rightly called the book that made our world, has inspired the best of Western civilization: science, technology, education and political and economic freedom. Because we are made in God's image, Christianity values human dignity and liberates those who are often marginalized in other cultures: slaves, women, children and outcasts.

4. Christianity's primary doctrine is that all of the worshiper's sins/wrongdoings, including those past, present and future have been paid for by God himself, and such a pardon as a gift from God accepted once by faith in His Son, Jesus, who paid the penalty for such sins by his death on the Cross. Whereas all other religions

require good works and religious activity of the worshipers to gain a pardon for the worshipers' sins.

5. Christianity is unique in that it expresses and believes there is, inside the Godhead, an all-embracing, self-giving, dynamic love between Father, Son, and Holy Spirit, so it can be truly said, "God is Love". Mankind feels the need for a power beyond itself but often defines that from man's finitude. Mankind makes images, fashions theologies to negotiate and "cut" deals with God developing rituals which often misrepresent God. Christianity represents God as all-powerful, all knowing, present everywhere, whose Nature is Love, who redeems and empowers those who accept and trust God's Grace (i.e. salvation in Jesus Christ).

6. Christian Faith is not man-made, but God revealed! Therefore, of universal validity, based on the conviction of the deity, authority and exclusive claims of the historic Christ as revealed in the Bible, Christ was (and is) Himself the message. The answer to the fundamental question of all religions, "Can I know God? What is He like?" has been given in the life, death and resurrection of the Lord Jesus Christ, for the barrier of sin which separates man from God is removed. It is just here that Christianity is unique! Other religions teach what man must do. Christianity alone tells what God has already done in Christ.

7. Two phrases differentiate Christianity from all other world religions; "in order that" and "because of." 'In order that' you can gain favor with God, you must keep ALL the rituals and make ALL the sacrifices. The reality is that in other religions you never know if or when you have done enough. Whereas, with Christianity, 'because of' Jesus Christ *[Ephesians 2:8]*, you can have a relationship

and peace with God, have your sins forgiven, receive the gift of eternal life and have the absolute certainty of Heaven *[John 14:6 and 1 John 5:12]*. World religions are man made. Christianity is God Inspired.

The common theme through the seven perspectives, which were provided by distinguished Church pastors, Bible teachers, and Christian Authors, is Jesus Christ the resurrected Savior. He is the only way to peace with God, eternal life and Heaven. They also underscore the Sovereignty of God, the Truth of the Bible and God's plan of Redemption for sinners, the Cross of Christ.

THE BRIDGE

The Bible lays out two outcomes for each of us: 1) eternal damnation and total separation from God and all that is good 2) eternal life in the presence of God free from all that is evil. Imagine a world where there is no pain, no guilt, no shame, no suffering—where a peace greater than any known on earth is forever. Each of us has a choice as to where we want to spend eternity. The following illustration helps to explain what God has done to make the second outcome possible. Here a cross bridges the gulf separating man from God.

That cross represents the Cross on which Jesus died. On that Cross, Jesus allowed himself to be separated from his father, God, and took on the sins of every man and woman who ever lived and who will ever live. He offered his life as a substitute for the lives of all. After his death, Jesus was buried and came back to life ushering in an eternal future in the presence of God for all who accept the sacrifice that Jesus made on their behalf. This sacrifice is a free gift. Nothing you can do would be enough to cover your sins—to make you clean enough—to enter God's presence and enjoy him forever. God only asks that you acknowledge that you are a sinner, repent of your sins, believe what Jesus did for you on the Cross and ask Him to become the lord of your life.

Paul, an apostle of Jesus, described this so clearly in a letter he wrote to the Christians in Rome in the years following the death and resurrection of Jesus.

If you declare with your mouth, "Jesus is Lord," and believe in your heart that God raised him from the dead, you will be saved. For it is with your heart that you believe and are justified, and it is with your mouth that you profess your faith and are saved.

[Romans 10:9 and 10]

Let's look closely at the illustration.

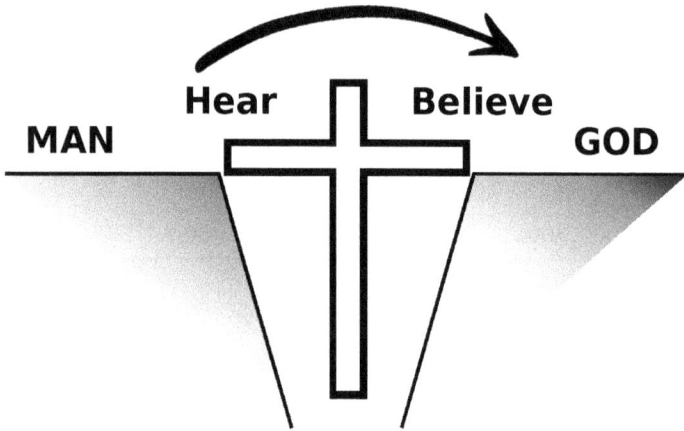

1. CROSSING OVER TO ETERNAL LIFE

Hear the Message, Believe in Christ (to believe is to entrust yourself to) and He promises (1) Eternal Life, (2) No Judgment and (3) that we will Cross Over from Death (Man's Side) to Life (God's Side) [John 5:24].

2. MAN HAS A PROBLEM

Man does not measure up to God's Character. God is Holy... Man is a sinner. God is Eternal... Man dies. God is Judge... Man is under the judgment of God [Romans 3:23; 6:23 and Hebrews 9:27].

3. MAN'S RESPONSE TO GOD'S SOLUTION

In order to receive the benefit of God's Solution, each of us must repent of our sins, believe that Jesus Christ already paid the price for those sins, [John 1:12] and then pray to the Lord and seek His salvation [Romans 10:13].

4. GOD HAS A SOLUTION TO MAN'S PROBLEM

God is Love. God demonstrated His love by sending His Son to die on the Cross for our sins [Look at Romans 5:8]. Christ the God-Man is the mediator between God and Man [See 1 Timothy 2:5].

5. GOD'S CHARACTER

God is the originator and sustainer of all that exists. God is Holy (Perfect), God is Eternal, God is Judge and God is Love. God is Truth. God is Life. God is Light.

ARE YOU READY TO CROSS OVER?

Will you Cross over from death to life? Call on the name of the Lord to be saved. [Romans 10:13] Pray to God like this:

God you are holy, eternal and the judge of all people. I am a sinner under the sentence of death and under your judgment. I believe that Jesus came to save me from eternal judgment. Father, I put my faith and trust in the death of your son, Jesus, to save me from the penalty of my sin. I praise you for your love for me and for the free gift of forgiveness through Jesus Christ.

• • • • • • • • • • • • • •

These "Tools", The Gospel and Next Steps, have been included in the Toolbox to enable you to provide a simple answer to two frequent questions you are likely to encounter in a conversation about life and faith matters.

A non-believer will often ask, "What is the Gospel?" and "What must I do to become a Believer and follower of Jesus?" Having a clear response is important. Like a good Scout, you will want to be prepared.

THE GOSPEL

The gospel is the good news that Jesus Christ, the Son of God, died for our sins and was resurrected. He eternally triumphed over his enemies, Satan, death, Hell, the grave and Satan's lies and deceit. Therefore, there is eternal life in him and no condemnation for those who believe, but only everlasting joy and the certainty of Heaven *[Romans 3:23, 5:1-8, 6:23, 10:9-11,13 and 1 John 5:12]*.

The Cross of Christ is the bridge between sinful man and a Holy God for all who put their Faith and Trust in Jesus as Lord and Savior. It is the only way to gain eternal life, peace with God and find the real meaning and purpose for life, i.e., those works prepared by God for each person before the foundation of the world.

A SINNER'S PRAYER OF CONFESSION

Lord Jesus, I confess I am a sinner in need of a Savior. I admit I have broken your Commandments. I invite you now into my heart as my Savior and Lord of my life. I commit to repent from my sinful ways and thoughts and follow you all the days of my life. I believe in my heart that you died on the Cross to pay the penalty for my sins. I believe that you are the resurrected Messiah, the Son of God, and are now seated at God's right hand interceding for me right now. I thank you, God, for your amazing grace that's saved a sinner like me. Amen!

If what you just prayed is the real intent of your heart, then you can be assured of your salvation and eternal life. 1 John 5:11 says, "He who has the son has life." This is a guarantee from God Himself. You are about to begin the most exciting adventure of your life. You will find your true calling and life's meaning and purpose as you live in peace with God and share your new testimony with everyone you meet. You are truly 'born again' and a new creation in Christ. It doesn't get any better than that.

The Bridge illustration shown has been included in the Toolbox to help you visualize, understand and explain the situation mankind is in due to our sinful nature. It can be used to initiate a discussion on the "Way" to cross over the Bridge to God. Remember that there is no path to God, but there is a 'Way', the Cross of Jesus Christ.

YOUR NEXT STEPS IN YOUR FAITH JOURNEY

First, share this exciting news with family, friends and everyone you encounter. Spread the Good News of Jesus Christ with those you meet.

Next, begin reading your Bible daily. Start with the Gospel of John to get a first hand account of the life of Jesus. Read a daily devotional.

Then attend a Christ centered, Bible teaching church, join a Bible study and use you talents to serve God!

LIST OF REASONS TO FOLLOW JESUS

This list is included here as it is one way to present the value of becoming a believer and a disciple maker. It points out the many benefits of following Jesus. He offers everyone who trusts in him the certainty of a life-transforming, personal and intimate relationship. It is the 'Good News' of the best way to live and the only way to die. A relationship with Jesus brings peace with God.

1. To gain salvation and eternal life.

2. To discover the meaning and purpose of life.

3. To discover one's true calling and be a humble servant leader. (Example: Jesus washing the disciples' feet example.)

4. To experience real joy and love in human relations.

5. To gain wisdom and understanding and discernment.

6. To find the strength and encouragement to live life with a passion.

7. To acquire perseverance, build moral character and acquire core values that guide one's decisions.

8. To live by the 10 Commandments so that you love and honor God and do not harm yourself or others.

9. To receive forgiveness for your sins and to be purified from all unrighteousness.

10. To be able to flee from temptations.

11. To not be deceived by Satan's lies, "Did God really say?...".

12. To be able to contend for and defend the Christian faith, to know the history of nations; why they rise and fall. The future of our Republic depends on it.

13. To know how to live in obedience to God's commands and to enjoy His presence now and for eternity.

14. To know the great men and women of the Faith and learn from their examples.

15. To know and claim the Bible's Promises for the children of God.

16. To have a Life transforming, personal, intimate and eternal relationship with Jesus.

PROPHETIC SCRIPTURES - JESUS THE PROMISED MESSIAH

There are two frequently asked questions by skeptics or seekers about Jesus. One question is, "Was Jesus the promised Messiah?" The second question is, "Are there prophecies about Jesus confirming that he is the Messiah and the Son of God?"

Before these questions can be answered, we must first recognize that the Bible is the only prophetic book that is 100% accurate and totally reliable. Why? It is God's inspired word and only God knows the future as He exists outside of time and space. In fact, God sees all of time from the beginning to the end of human history as if it is already an accomplished fact.

There are more than 300 specific prophecies in the Bible regarding Jesus's first and second coming. Most of these prophecies were made hundreds of years before Jesus's birth.

1. *[Genesis 3:15 and Isaiah 7:14]* – The Messiah was to be the seed of a woman (virgin birth)

2. *[Micah 5:2]* – Born in Bethlehem, Ephrathah (the city of King David's birth)

3. *[Isaiah 53:1]* – His rejection by ruling Jews of Jesus' Day.

4. *[Psalm 22:14-17]* – Jesus to die by crucifixion (not a method of killing until the Romans introduced it 1000 years later)

5. *[Isaiah 53:5-12]* – The Messiah, Jesus, to die as a sacrifice for sin (The Cross)

6. *[Psalm 22:18]* – Garments divided by the Roman soldiers

7. *[Psalm 16:10]* – the Messiah to be resurrected confirming that he had conquered both sin and death. (After the resurrection, He was seen by over 500 people during His 40 days on earth, including the 11 disciples before He ascended to Heaven. The Event that Changed the world!)

Many skeptics and atheists have tried to prove that Jesus was not the Son of God or the promised Messiah. Among those are men like C.S. Lewis, Lee Strobel, Josh McDowell, Don Bierle, and Frank Morrison, a very gifted English lawyer who set out to write a book that was going to be titled *Disproving the Resurrection of Jesus*. When Morrison completed his extensive research, he was convinced by the rules of evidence that confirmed Jesus's resurrection, and he himself became a Follower, as did the others mentioned above.

These are some ideas to consider in reference to these seven prophecies. First, a virgin birth is a miracle that only God can accomplish. Secondly, no one gets to choose the place of their birth. Thirdly no one gets to choose their parents or their ancestral line. In addition, no one knows or chooses the city their parents will live in. Jesus was known as a Nazarene because Mary and Joseph settled in Nazareth, another prophecy fulfilled. It is also a fact that no one knows how they will die, especially by crucifixion. Finally, Jesus was the first to be resurrected as a foreshadowing for all those who would put their faith and trust in Jesus as their personal Lord and Savior.

• • • • • • • • • • • • •

These are some final thoughts on the evidence and facts for Jesus as the promised Messiah and Son of God. The probability of any one person fulfilling even these six prophecies is so great that it would be impossible unless it was orchestrated by God before the beginning of time, as his plan of redemption of humankind. The evidence is in. Jesus is the Messiah, The Son of God, who died on a Cross as a sacrifice for sin and is the only promised Redeemer for all who would trust him as Lord and Savior.

Note: *For a longer list of Prophecies, see pages 186 and 187 in the book* Answers to Your Greatest Questions, *by Jack Dannemiller.*

CHAPTER 7

TOOLS IN THE TOOLBOX

Every craftsman has a Toolbox with the tools they need to apply their trade.

It is no different for Christian Disciple Makers. They must have a variety of tools available to be equipped to present God's truth to those seeking reasons to follow Jesus. The tools start first with a thorough knowledge of the Scriptures. Then, there are the 'mental' tools, or 'soft' tools, which appear in the manual itself. There are the tools from history, science, and the Bible including knowledge, evidence, facts, and truths. You will notice the Art of Dialogue tools - how to engage the other person in the conversation. Then, there are the apologetics tools - how to respond to the other person's questions (What and Why). Next, there are the Prophecy tools - Jesus the Messiah. Lastly, there are the Reasons tools - Why follow Jesus, What Christian parents want for their children, What God wants for His children (believers), and, finally, Creation vs. Evolution arguments.

In addition, it is most often necessary to have tools, handouts, to use that show the other person what you were talking about, i.e., the features and benefits of becoming a Christian. In this toolbox there are these five "Tools" for you to choose from, or the 'hard' tools, shown below. With practice you will learn to use them like a 'Master' craftsman.

- *Answers to Life's Greatest Questions* Booklet
- *Light of the World* Booklet
- **The Gospel & Next Steps to Sanctification Bookmark**
- **Pathway to Heaven Bookmark**
- **Bridge Illustration Handout**

These tools are available for purchase online, direct from livingdialog.org. The booklets can also be previewed on our website lifesbasicquestions.com. As purchasers of the Disciple Makers Toolbox, you are entitled to purchase any of the above at regular price and receive a second one free. For churches and other Christian Ministry Organizations, discounts are available. Finally, there are the reference tools for the journey to spiritual maturity. They are found in the Appendix and include our ministries' four disciple making studies, the book *Answers To Your Greatest Questions*, the book *To Know with Certainty*, and a list of other disciple making resources including, of course, a good study Bible like the NIV: Life Application Study Bible, Third Edition.

◆

Truths or 'Gems of Wisdom' about
redemption, salvation and the Christian
Life are all found in the Bible.
Hidden treasures to be discovered!

◆

CHAPTER 8

DISCIPLESHIP RESOURCES & REFERENCES PRESENTED IN THE BOOK

SUGGESTED METHOD TO EXPLORE, LIFE APPLICATION BIBLE*

This study method is included in the Toolbox because it has proven both to lead seekers to a personal relationship with Jesus as their Savior and to educate disciples in the Scriptures. It will direct your attention to the Truths or 'Gems of Wisdom' that are contained in the Bible with a focus on the books of the New Testament. In particular, truths about redemption, salvation and the Christian life journey that are not often apparent or understood by just a casual reading of the Scriptures, come alive in the *Life Application Bible*.

As a testimony to the effectiveness of this method, I am going to share a brief story about a friend and colleague, Sam, who I have discipled for over a year. Sam has been battling cancer for the past five years, visiting M.D. Anderson Cancer Center in Houston every three months. While he had been attending church, he did not know Jesus as his savior or that salvation is only by God's Grace alone, through Faith alone, in Christ alone. Sam reached out to me to help him 'know for certain' that when he died he would go to heaven and have eternal life.

*NIV: Life Application Study Bible, Third Edition

As we met regularly by phone and communicated through text messages, he got answers to his questions about life and faith and eternity. Six months into our discipling process he committed his life to Jesus and now has Peace with God and the assurance of Heaven. The truth in the Gospel of John and the book of Romans opened his heart to the prompting of the Holy Spirit. Sam is no longer anxious about the things of the world or his eternal destiny. Yes, he is still battling cancer but has assurance that God is with him and will never leave him or forsake him.

What Sam experienced, so can all who want to become a Christian. And, for everyone who wants to be a better disciple maker, following the method shown below is guaranteed to help in that endeavor. Remember, God has promised to reveal himself to those who earnestly seek Him and believe that He exists. That means that anyone who faithfully, sincerely and seriously spends quality time studying the Bible and praying for understanding and discernment of the Scriptures, will encounter God as never before.

Follow this method yourself so that you can share with others how it has helped you in your personal faith journey. Your work as a disciple-maker is made easier when you share your personal testimony. And your recommendation of this Bible-study method will have much more impact when you let others know that you have already done it. So, when you speak to others, you will have confidence when you say: "I urge you to use this study method wisely and enjoy your journey through the Scriptures with Jesus. I believe that as you study, you will surely come to know Him as the Son of God, the returning King and your Savior and friend. I will pray that God will bless your reading and study of his Holy inspired Word."

Week 1 Read the Gospel of John - Before you start, ask God to reveal His truths to you as you read. God has promised to make Himself known to those who diligently seek Him. Read four to five chapters a day. Reflect on what you read during the week.

Week 2 Read the Gospel of John again - This time asking three questions as you read the chapters:
- What does it say? (literally)
- What does it mean?
- What does it say to me? (personally)

As you read each chapter this second week, read the footnotes as soon as you complete a chapter. The commentary in the *Life Application Bible* is like having a teacher right alongside you as you go. Actually, your tutor is God's Holy Spirit that will give you understanding and discernment of the Scriptures, God's Living Word.

Week 3 Read the introduction to the Gospel of John, the three pages that precede Chapter 1. This time as you read through the chapters, pay particular attention to what Jesus said about Himself. Who He was. Why He came. What He taught. What He promised. Jesus' words are in RED. You will also discover John's purpose for writing his Gospel. I think you will enjoy the brief biography of some of the main characters in this book.

Week 4 Go to the beginning of the New Testament and start reading through Mathew, Mark and Luke using the same process as outlined in steps 1, 2 and 3. If you keep at it, before long, you will understand God's gift of a Savior, Jesus, and why we all need one. I guarantee that once you start on this adventure, you will never want to turn back!

Knowing God through a personal relationship with Jesus Christ is the purpose for which we were created. God did not create religions, man did. God wants each person to experience an intimate daily walk with Him, a relationship. True Christianity is not about rites, rituals and meaningless sacrifices. Christianity is about God coming down to His creation and redeeming it back after Adam and Eve sinned and brought death on the human race. Religion is about mankind trying to justify itself before God by doing or not doing certain things. God made it so simple. Mankind tries to make it very complicated.

Somewhere during this process, you will encounter Jesus on a very personal basis. When you see who He really is, it will be easy to say yes to Him and invite Him into your life as your Savior and Lord. You will experience forgiveness, peace, love, joy and an abundant life like you would never have dreamed or enjoyed. Then gradually God will work on you as you mature in your faith to become the person He planned for you at your birth. It is never too late to start a personal relationship with Jesus. But, as my wife, Jean, and I discovered, the sooner, the better.

Walking day-by-day with Jesus is the best way to enjoy life while here on earth assured that you will soon be spending eternity with God. If you are still unsure why God wants you to know his Son, I suggest you look up the following

Scripture verses and ask yourself this question: "What does this mean to me?"

1. Read *Romans 3:23*
2. Read *Romans 6:23*
3. Read *John 3:3*

Then, ask yourself: "Why did Jesus come to die?"

4. Read *John 14:6*
5. Read *Romans 10:9-11*
6. Read *2 Corinthians 5:15*
7. Read *Romans 10:13*
8. Read *Revelation 3:20*

Finally, if you want forgiveness for your sins and believe that Jesus died on the Cross for you and rose again, then all you have to do is invite Him into your heart and your life. At that moment, God honors your request, and you have received eternal life and will begin life's most exciting adventure.

I know that this is a rather lengthy set of steps, but I assure you it's the best investment of time you will ever make. Once you become immersed in the Word, you will want to know more and more about this all-powerful, yet intimately personal God. You also will want to explore the rest of the New Testament and then go back and start on the Old Testament, beginning with Genesis.

WHAT DOES GOD WANT FOR HIS CHILDREN?

When we accept Jesus as Lord and Savior, we become children of God, beloved members of God's family and joint heirs with Jesus. That is truly amazing, but there is more. We gain all the rights and privileges of the royal family. As such, we will want to please and obey our Heavenly Father's expectations of us, just like our earthly parents expect from their children.

So the question we must ask is, "What does God want for His children?" We can certainly say for starters that he wants us to know Him personally, experience His love and enjoy His Presence now and forever. The list that follows is a biblical list of some of the more important expectations of God that we, as His children, should want to lovingly follow. Ultimately, God wants each of us to have the same character qualities as Jesus and live lives that honor and bring glory to Him.

Therefore, pray seriously that God will transform you by the power of the Holy Spirit into the likeness of Jesus. I urge you to use this list as a beginning reference to guide your transformation as you become a beloved child of God. One day when your mortal life ends, God will welcome you home to His celestial city with open arms and a big hug.

TRUST: In Him as Creator and Father of the Lord Jesus Christ. *[Genesis 1:1]*

BELIEVE: In Jesus as Lord and Savior. *[John 1:1-5, 1 John 5:12]*

LOVE: God and your neighbor as yourself. *[Luke 10:27]*

TRUTH: Know God's living Word, The Bible, and live it! Memorize it. *[John 14:6, John 8:32]*

SHARE: The Gospel – The Great Commission, as you are going about life each day. *[Matthew 28:19]*

OBEY: His Ten Commandments. *[Exodus 20]*

GRACE: Receive His salvation and blessings with gratitude. *[Ephesians 2:8]*

MERCY: Extend grace and mercy to others as God has shown His to you.

PURIFICATION: Daily seek to remove from your life those thoughts, comments and habits preventing you from becoming more like Jesus. Be made Righteous and Holy. *[John 1:9]*

SANCTIFICATION: Become more like Jesus every day in every way. *[Ephesians 1:4-6]*

QUIET TIME: Set aside time for a daily experience with God to fully and intimately know Him. A time of prayer and reflection will help you discern God's will, His good, pleasing and perfect will for your life *[Romans 12:2]*. Have time to let go and let God rule and reign in your life. A time to enjoy just being in God's presence, to experience fully His unfailing love, to be immersed in His Amazing Grace, to reflect on His promises, to be renewed by the Holy Spirit, to receive His 'marching orders' for the day and to commit to live life to Honor Him in everything.

WORSHIP: Regularly participate in worship services in a Christ-centered, gospel-preaching church. Join a small group Bible study. Attend a disciple-making Sunday school class. Become equipped to contend for and defend the reasons for your faith. Discover your God-given gifts and use them in His service to build God's kingdom; i.e., teach a Sunday school class, mentor youth, volunteer in the church office, go on mission trips, serve in a soup kitchen, et cetera. Be a faithful steward of your time, talents and treasures.

WHAT DO CHRISTIAN PARENTS WANT FOR THEIR CHILDREN?

Christian parents, true followers of Jesus Christ, want their children to also come to faith in Jesus. Why? There are many reasons, but the primary ones are that they will have a loving family unit on earth and be together for all eternity. Faith in God and in Jesus is undoubtedly the most important hope of parents, but of course, they want much more for their children. They want them to develop into mature, responsible, loving and considerate adults.

In this post-Christian era, parenting is a daunting challenge. The culture offers many temptations and attractions to lead children away from their faith. It creates doubts in their minds about matters such as the existence of God, the truth of the Scriptures, that Jesus is the Son of God, that heaven and hell are real places and much more. Given these challenges, it takes deliberate and constant effort and communication by parents to achieve the successful raising of their children. Remember, hope is not a method!

The following list was developed by interviewing Christian parents about their expectations, hopes and dreams for their children. It is included in the Toolbox as a guide and reference for parents as they raise, train, counsel, listen to, guide and pray for their children. We trust that you will find it a valuable tool for parenting and for making new disciples.

1. Faith in God, trust his word, hope for the future, heaven.

2. Believe in Jesus as Savior and Lord – eternal life.

3. Family being all together for eternity.

4. Know the Bible stories and heroes – when young.

5. Know about the heroes of faith *[Hebrews 11]*.

6. Learn how to pray – memorize Bible verses.

7. Have a tender heart filled with gratitude and thanksgiving for all God's blessings.

8. Retain a working conscience – know right from wrong and good from evil.

9. Acquire moral core values – honesty and integrity.

10. Maintain an impeccable character and reputation.

11. Emotional intelligence – self-awareness and impact on others.

12. Find their life calling that honors God.

13. Have a passion for sharing their faith.

14. Know contentment in all circumstances.

15. Advocacy – stand up for themselves, the less fortunate and righteous causes.

16. Appreciation for and protection of their physical and mental health. Recognize that their bodies are temples of the Holy Spirit.

17. Empathy – put others first – be compassionate, caring and loving.

18. Become lifelong learners – appreciate their education, read extensively to search for and know the truth.

19. Develop a Biblical worldview – become discerning.

20. Know Apologetics - what Christians believe and why they believe it.

21. That Church, pastors and teachers answer their questions to identify and overcome their skepticism and unbelief.

22. Participate in a team sport – learn the principles of teamwork.

23. Perform community service.

24. Go on at least one mission trip.

25. Identify and have a Christian mentor.

26. Have great relationships; deep, trusting, open, fun, life-sharing, dependable and transparent.

27. Participate in the youth ministry of the church and a Christian ministry like Young life, Fellowship of Christian Athletes or Athletes in Action.

28. Attend a Summit Ministry two-week summer camp in Colorado. Learn how to think and reason as a Christian.

29. Acquire good work habits and Christian work ethics.

Creating new disciples within a home is the most effective way to ensure that the Gospel continues through the ages. That's why parents (and grandparents/aunts/uncles) should diligently teach, guide and model Christ-centered behavior. If studies are to be believed, as much as 80% of what children learn comes through observation. That's why parents should continually do what they want their children to do. If you want them to read their Bibles, they need to see you reading and reverencing the Bible. If you want them to experience other cultures, you need to take them on mission trips, not just send them. If you want them to treat others with compassion and grace, they need to see you doing the same. There is no greater joy in life than to watch your children replicate your model of commitment to Christ and the Gospel.

CHRISTIAN APOLOGETICS: 101 STUDY GUIDE OUTLINE

The word apologetics is somewhat misleading and has nothing to do with apologizing in the modern sense of the word. Apologetics by definition is, "Reasoned arguments in justification of something, someone or a cause. Persuading with reason and evidence and truth." Christian apologetics is building the case for explaining and defending the Christian faith. It can be summarized as follows: "*What Christians believe and why Christians believe it.*"

First, an examination of the '*What is believed*' includes knowledge about the existence and character of God, creation, nature, origins of man, sin, morality, stewardship, life's purpose, Jesus Christ, redemption, salvation, Heaven, Hell, the Christian church, the Bible, Prophecy, the Old Testament history of nations, End Times and eternity.

The second part of Christian Apologetics is '*Why Christians believe it.*' Christians start with the belief that the Bible is the inspired Word of God and, therefore, what we read accurately reflects the character of God, His creation, and His desire to enter into a relationship with the greatest of His creation--mankind. It also reliably explains man's breaking of that relationship and God's plan of redemption, leading to the restoration of the original relationship through Jesus' death and resurrection. They trust the evidence that proves the Bible is historically correct, that it is the best-documented of all ancient books and that it contains a prophecy that is 100% accurate as only God could see the future of human history as if it is already completed. The Bible is a miracle in its own right as it was written over a period of 1,500 years by 40 authors in complete harmony and without any unexplainable contradictions.

Christians trust and believe the evidence of both biblical and secular records (including those of Josephus AD 38-97 and Tacitus AD 56-113) of the life, teaching, miracles, death by crucifixion, resurrection (witnessed by over 500 people), and ascension to heaven of Jesus Christ. They further believe the evidence of the dramatically transformed lives of Jesus' 12 disciples, who boldly proclaimed the truth of the gospel and were martyred for their testimonies. Then there is the miraculous contribution of Christianity to Western Civilization; literature, art, science, music, mathematics, medicine, education, philosophy, law and much more.

Finally, there are the witness and testimonies of the hundreds of millions of followers of Jesus Christ through the centuries. Why so many believers? The answer is because Jesus is the only way to eternal life and a transformed life full of meaning and purpose. He is 'The Way' to receive God's gifts of joy, love, peace, forgiveness, contentment, faith, and eternal hope.

In summary, Christian apologetics means to make a reasoned case for:

1. The existence of God

2. The intelligent design of Creation

3. Jesus Christ the promised Messiah, the Son of God and the only way to Heaven and Eternal Life

4. That Jesus is coming back as "King of Kings and Lord of Lords"

5. That there will be a Judgment Day of God

6. The Bible is the inspired Word of God

7. That Heaven and Hell are real places

8. In Christian terms, apologetics is:

   a. WHAT Christians Believe

   b. WHY They Believe It

   c. WHY Their Belief is True

   d. WHY It's Important

There are entire books that provide in-depth examinations of apologetics. In this book we have provided this condensed version so that Christian Apologetics can be easily understood and even memorized so that every disciple of Jesus will have a ready response for those requiring an explanation of the beliefs Christians hold as truths to live by and are even willing to die for.

However, after the Apostles Creed that follows, for those disciples who want to be more thoroughly equipped in the subject of apologetics, we have included an expanded version, Apologetics 201 and a summary of the Apologetics of Jesus from the book by Norman L. Geisler and Patrick Zukeran.

THE APOSTLES' CREED

The Apostles' Creed is a good starting point as a summary of what Christians believe. It is well worth remembering and memorizing. In some ways, it's much like our Pledge of Allegiance to the flag. It is a concise statement of the Christian's allegiance to God.

I believe in God,
The Father Almighty,
Creator of Heaven and earth.

I believe in Jesus Christ, His only Son, our Lord,
Who was conceived by the Holy Spirit
And born of the Virgin Mary,
He suffered under Pontius Pilate,
Was crucified, died and was buried;
He descended to Hell.
The third day he rose again from the dead;
He ascended into Heaven
And sitteth at the right hand of God,
the Father Almighty,
From thence He will come
To judge the living and the dead.

I believe in the Holy Spirit,
The Holy Christian Church,
The Communion of Saints,
The Forgiveness of Sins,
The Resurrection of the Body,
And the Life Everlasting.

AMEN.

CHRISTIAN APOLOGETICS: 201 STUDY GUIDE OUTLINE

Christian apologetics is building the case for explaining and defending the Christian faith. Simply stated, apologetics defines what Christians believe, why Christians believe it, and why it's important to know. In this study, it is defined as the discipline of offering a defense of, or case for, or evidence for, the veracity and reliability of the Christian faith.

Session 1 - Reasons why it's important for all Christians.
- Christians should be able to explain why they have faith in Jesus.
- Christians should be able to critique unbiblical worldviews.
- Christians should use their minds and intellect to the glory of God. Following Jesus does not mean turning your brain off, rather it means giving your heart, your mind and your soul to Him.
- Christians throughout history have used apologetics.
- Christian apologetics answers the questions of non-Christians and removes the distractions from belief.
- Apologetics and evangelism point non-Christians to faith in Jesus.

Session 2 – The focus on the existence of God.
- Probability: every day, we exercise faith, and it is reasonable to have faith in the supernatural.
- Creation and design: intelligent design is more intellectually plausible than creation by random chance.
- Anthropic arguments: things about ourselves – conscience, capacity for good and evil, desiring eternal

life and faith experiences are best explained by the existence of God.

- Immaterialism: The existence of love, compassion and beauty demonstrate that we do not live in a simply materialistic universe.
- Transcendental argument: Knowledge, logic and science are only possible because God's existence is a precondition for all thinking, knowledge and wisdom.
- God is the Being greater than that which cannot be conceived. Therefore God exists!

Session 3: We deal with the problem of evil. The big question for unbelievers is: How can God be all powerful or all good if evil exists in the world?

- There is no perfect resolution to this issue for Christians. We are not God, our knowledge is limited and our minds are not perfect.
- Many things in life are still a mystery. The complete answer to this question has not been revealed to us. However, we trust God for what we do know and what God has revealed to us. When in God's presence one day, we will see things from his perspective and may understand more fully.
- As Christians, we do know the following:
  - God is the all-powerful governor of the universe.
  - God is in control of every aspect of his creation.
  - God is never blameworthy for the evil that occurs. Those who commit evil are to blame. Men have free will to make their own choices--good or bad, wise or unwise.
  - God is always good and holy, and He hates evil.

- God judges us. We do not judge Him. As Christians, we need to remember that God's ultimate purpose is not to provide happiness for man but rather that man enters into an intimate personal relationship with Him through his son Jesus Christ. Man's chief purpose is to glorify God, honor Him with his life and work, trust God in all things and enjoy His presence now and forever.

Finally, Christians know from the Bible that God will one day put an end to pain, suffering and all evil *[Revelation 14:6]*. The question of evil will be resolved!

Session 4 – We explore why Christians believe the Bible is true.
- The Bible came from God, by the Holy Spirit, through men to mankind. The New Testament is of Apostolic origin, meaning being attributed to and based on the preaching and teaching of the first generation of apostles or their close companions.
- The Bible is the ultimate standard of truth. Christians put their faith in the author of the Bible, Jesus Christ and believe the Bible to be true because it is God's Word.
- Christians believe in the Bible because the New Testament documents are historically reliable and verifiable. After all, Jesus' character is shown to be trustworthy and both the Old and New Testament books were and are the Word of God.
- The Bible is the best documented of all ancient books. The New Testament was written between A.D. 40-100 when most of the apostles were still living.

- The Bible is a miracle in its own right, as it was written over a period of 1,500 years by 40 authors in complete harmony without any unexplainable contradictions. The Bible contains prophecies that are 100% accurate because only God can see the future of human history as if it is already completed. God is not bound by time.

- The Bible, being historically correct, documents life, teachings, miracles, death by crucifixion, resurrection (500+ witnesses), and the ascension to heaven of Jesus Christ. Jesus was a real historical figure also documented by historians of the time, including Josephus (AD 38-97) and Tacitus (AD 56-113).

Finally, when unbelievers raise objections to the Bible's truth or reliability, the best response is not to argue but to open the Word of God and have them read it aloud. The word of God is powerful in its own right for explaining human nature and truth.

Why read aloud? Faith comes from hearing the Word and Truth of God. You will need to know the scriptures that outline God's plan for redemption and salvation. In other words, the Good News of the Bible, is that salvation for sinners is by God's Grace alone, through Faith alone, in Jesus alone. There is no other name under Heaven by which you may be saved [Acts 4:12].

Session 5 – The Resurrection of Jesus Christ.
The primary question is, Why do you believe a dead man arose from his tomb? This is the fundamental question of Christianity. It is the foundation upon which the gospel is based and on which the church was established. It is in Jesus's resurrection that all

who believe in him have the hope and assurance of eternal life and Heaven. It is the most extraordinary event in all of human history. Let's find out why it is True! The key points of this lesson follow:

- Jesus is a big deal: all of Christianity rests upon the life, death and resurrection of Christ.
- Jesus was a historical person, as we saw in Session 4.
- Jesus is the point of the history of Israel. God worked through history to point them towards a Messiah. His Story begins in the book of Genesis, continues in the Psalms and the prophets and climaxes in the 'fullness of time' with the birth of Jesus. We will hit the highlights of the story in this session.
- Here is a summary of what happened in Jesus's last days:

  Arrested in the garden > trials by Pontius Pilate > torture and humiliation > walk to Calvary > crucifixion > death > darkness from noon till 3 PM > placed in a tomb > sealed with a large stone and a Roman seal > 3 days of silence > the empty tomb > the resurrected Jesus appears to Mary Magdalene and the 11 disciples > Jesus spends 40 days on the earth and is seen by over 500 people > He returned to the Mount of Olives > He gives the disciples the Great Commission, and in their presence, they witness his ascension to heaven > the disciples are empowered by the Holy Spirit to spread the Gospel > except for John, they all died a martyrs death for the truth they knew > the world is changed forever.

There will be those who question the resurrection even though it is one of the best-documented events in all history. The evidence of its impact on the world is a testimony to the fact of Jesus' resurrection. Other significant historical changes took place as a result of this event.

Some are:

- The day of rest for the Christianized world was changed from Saturday to Sunday.
- Communion was introduced to the believers (the church) as a regular remembrance that the body of Jesus was broken for them, and his blood was shed for the remission of their sins
- The calendar was eventually changed.
- The history of Western civilization was dramatically impacted because of Jesus' resurrection and the church of believers.

Session 6 - We conclude the study of apologetics with a review of World Religions.

We will spend our time today learning how to engage with people from some of the world's largest religions – Hinduism, Buddhism and Islam. We will explore the teachings of these religions briefly and answer three questions:

1. Don't all religions teach the same thing?
2. Is Jesus the only way to peace with God and eternal life?
3. What about those who have never heard about Jesus?

There are three categories of religion:

- **Monotheism** - There is one God: Christianity, Judaism, and Islam.

- **Polytheism** - There are many gods: Hinduism, Eastern religions.
- **Pantheism** - All is God, God is in all: Buddhism, Animism.

We will now briefly look at some of the facts, policies and differences in some major religions.

Islam – means submission to God, and followers are Muslims. It was founded by Mohammed in 622 AD, who believed he was the final messenger through whom Allah (God) revealed the faith to the world. Islam is more than just a religious belief. It is a system that governs all aspects of life, including commerce, government, personal behavior, and religious rituals.

Beliefs in Islam and contrasts with Christianity will be discussed in this session. Some questions to address include, Is the Bible God's word? What is the purpose of God's revelation? Did Jesus die on the Cross? What about the Trinity? Muslims do not believe in an incarnate God that you can know personally.

Hinduism – there is no single idea of God. It is a works-based religion. Karma is the debt of one's bad actions, and so every soul is trapped in a cycle of birth and then death. Rebirth is the belief in reincarnation.

For Hindus, history is a cycle, not linear. Therefore, Hinduism teaches a life cycle of meaninglessness. Hinduism replaces resurrection with reincarnation and both grace and faith with works. Hindus believe in Jesus as a divine manifestation, but no more special than any others. Question for Hindus,

How do you know when you're good enough to be liberated and escape the cycle? You can't! Salvation is not possible.

Buddhism – teaches that we all are God – God is in all of us all of us. Buddhism has no omnipotent, creator God who exists apart from this or any other universe. Buddhists also believe in karma – the cause-and-effect that traps souls in an endless cycle of birth and rebirth. Buddhism teaches "Four Noble Truths."

These are:
1. To live is to suffer.
2. Suffering is caused by desire/being attached to things.
3. One can eliminate suffering by accepting fate.
4. Desire is eliminated by following the path to Nirvana, where all action and interaction ceases. It is a state of enlightenment and the place where personality is extinguished.

The question is, how can a Buddhist be saved from the meaninglessness of their founder who said, "There is no external savior, it is up to each of you to work out your own liberation. Take refuge in yourself."?

Some more questions to close this session:
1. Don't all religions teach the same thing? The answer is no.
2. Is Jesus the only way? The answer is yes. He said so himself *[John 14:6]*.
3. Is it arrogant to claim Jesus is the only way? No. It is the truth from God's Word. And the invitation is open to all who believe. Therefore Christianity is the most inclusive of all religions.

4. If Jesus is the only way, then other religions would be false. That is true. They are false.
5. Is it enough to be sincere in what you believe, or is the object of your belief more important? It is not sincerity but the details of the religion that makes a difference. In Christianity, it is the details and Jesus himself which make salvation and eternal life worthy and, therefore, the other religions worth nothing.

Finally, the familiar objection by unbelievers, what about those who have never heard the good news of Jesus?

The answer from the Bible is that all humankind is already under God's judgment because all men and women have sinned and fallen short of the glory of God *[Romans 3:23]*, and are therefore already morally accountable to God and must give an answer to Him. They have the witness of Creation, the conscience within them and their own culpability for their personal sins. The Good News is that all who call upon the name of the Lord will be saved *[Romans 10:9-10]*.

THE APOLOGETICS OF JESUS

By Norman L. Geisler and Patrick Zukeran
Edited and adapted for Small Group Study By JCD

The historical use of apologetics, reasoned arguments and justification of something, someone or a cause, goes back to the time of the Greeks and Socrates. It became known as the Socratic Method, persuading with reason and evidence. Jesus used apologetics to establish his credentials as the prophesied Messiah, the Son of Man and the Son of God. As we might expect, Jesus is a 'Grand Master' of apologetics. He employed all of its techniques to make a case for himself and his cause, i.e., to establish the Kingdom of God and bring it to a fallen and sinful world.

This brief look at the apologetics of Jesus which follows is included in the toolbox so that his disciples can learn from his example. [Note: More details can be found in the referenced book, *The Apologetics of Jesus: A Caring Approach to Dealing with Doubters* by Norman L. Geisler and Patrick Zukeran; 2009; Baker Books]

1. Jesus' use of testimony - Witnesses to the events
   a. John the Baptist - "The lamb of God that takes away the sins of the world." *[John 1:29]*
   b. God the Father - "My beloved Son in whom I am we pleased." *[Mark 1:11, Matthew 3:17 and 5:17]*
   c. Miracles, Works and Signs – "No one could perform the signs you are doing if God were not with him." *[John 3:2]*
   d. Scripture -Prophecies of the Messiah -Fulfill the Law, Prophets and Psalms *[Matthew 5:17]*

e. Moses – Moses wrote the Law given by God, and Jesus

f. The testimony of a sinless life - Jesus' perfect life demonstrates his testimony is true. *[John 8:41, 46, 52]*

Therefore, in making his case that he is the Messiah and the Son of God, Jesus gives reasons and evidence, i.e., Apologetics -The use of testimony!

2. Jesus used miracles to verify his claim as the Son of God.
    a. Creation, human life, Mosaic period (Egypt) verified Moses was God's person.
    b. Prophets – God's messengers about God's acts of Divine judgment. *[John 10:24, 25, 38]*
    c. Apostles Miracles

Jesus' miracles confirm his claim to be the son of God and the authority over every realm of nature. He created everything including the laws that govern it but was not subject to them, i.e., walks on water, calms the storms, feeds the 5,000, raises the dead, etc.

Remember, if God exists, miracles are possible, i.e., they are supernatural special acts of God. Acts that offer many infallible proofs of Jesus' claim.

3. Jesus' resurrection - A verifiable proven historical event – over 500 witnesses plus the 11 Apostles and the dramatic conversion of Paul, i.e., "resurrected to a new creation in Christ."

4. Jesus' use of reason - He used all the laws of logical reasoning. God said, "Come let us reason together." Jesus reasoned with the authorities and confounded them with his wisdom, which was far superior to theirs.

5. Jesus' use of parables — They taught valuable lessons and were memorable:
   a. The Good Samaritan
   b. The Prodigal son
   c. Parables illustrate truth through stories. Jesus was the greatest storyteller that ever lived. Remember His "I Am" statements:
      i. Bread of Life
      ii. Light of the world
      iii. Gate for the sheep
      iv. The Good Shepherd
      v. The Resurrection and the Life
      vi. The Way, the Truth and the Life
      vii. The True Vine
      viii. Prince of Peace

6. Jesus' use of prophecy — The fulfillment of Old Testament prophecies. Over 100 of His first coming.

7. Jesus' use of Arguments for God
   a. Cosmological – First Cause, a beginning must have beginner, God!
   b. Anthropological – Human beings made in the image of God are able to think and reason. Humans have an inner sense to worship. God has placed eternity in the hearts of mankind.
   c. Theological – Nature itself and its incredibly Intelligent Design. Something only God could do.
   d. The Moral Argument – knowledge of good and evil, right and wrong – Conscience – The source of objective morality, God!

FINAL THOUGHTS: Even though Jesus was the greatest apologist of all time, he affirmed that no person can be brought to God without the ministry of the Holy Spirit. It is the Holy Spirit who convinces people of sin and the need for a Savior and brings about conversion.

Neither reason nor evidence alone was or is sufficient to bring about faith. To believe in Christ is the work of God, but, evidence, truth and facts, i.e., apologetics, can be the means by which the work of the Holy Spirit produces salvation in a person's life. That's why Christian apologetics is important for disciples to use in presenting the Gospel.

MY FRIEND POEM

This poem has purposely been placed on the last page as a reminder and motivator for you to be a faithful disciple of Jesus, who fearlessly and confidently shares the Gospel with friends, family, neighbors and colleagues. Resources have been identified and suggested for your study, and tools provided so that you can become equipped with the soul-saving 'Words of Life' and with the essentials of the dialogue process necessary to accomplish the mission. The mission is to be about Jesus' Great Commission given for all believers as you are going about your daily life.

In other words, tell everyone in your 'world' the Good News that the only way to heaven and eternal life is by faith in Jesus Christ *[Ephesians 2:8]*. I encourage you to make as your motto the statement found in *Romans 1:16*, "I will not be ashamed of the gospel of Christ for it is the power of God unto salvation for all who believe."

When you obey Jesus' command, you can know for certain that one day when you are face-to-face with Jesus, you'll hear the best praise ever, "Well done, good and faithful servant, enter into the joy prepared for you before the foundation of the world." *[Matthew 25:34]*

MY FRIEND
D. J. Higgins

My friend, I stand in judgment now
And feel that you're to blame somehow
While on this earth I walked with you day by day
And never did you point the way

You knew the Lord in truth and glory
But never did you tell the story
My knowledge then was very dim
You could have led me safe to Him

Though we lived together here on earth
You never told me of your second birth
And now I stand this day condemned
Because you failed to mention Him

You taught me many things, that's true
I called you friend and trusted you
But now I learned, now it's too late
You could have kept me from this fate

We walked by day and talked by night
And yet you showed me not the light
You let me live, and love and die
And all the while you knew I'd never live on high

Yes, I called you friend in life
And trusted you in joy and strife
Yet in coming to this end
I see you really weren't my friend

APPENDIX - SUPPLEMENTAL RESOURCES & REFERENCES

- *NIV - Life Application Bible* - Zondervan
- *The MacArthur Bible Commentary* - John MacArthur
- Books for finding Evidence, Truth and Answers:
  - *To Know with Certainty* – Lee Southard, PhD (www.ToKnowWithCertainty.com)
  - *Answers to Your Greatest Questions* – John (Jack) Dannemiller (www.LivingDialog.org)
  - *Mere Christianity* - C. S. Lewis
  - *Case for Christ* - Lee Strobel
  - *Reflections on the Existence of God: A Series of Essays* - Richard E. Simmons III
  - *Face to Face with Jesus* - Randy Alcorn
  - *Trusting God: Even When Life Hurts* - Jerry Bridges
  - *The New Evidence That Demands a Verdict: Fully Updated* - Josh McDowell

NOTE: *Book resources are available from Christian Booksellers, Christianbook.com, Amazon.com, Barnesandnoble.com, LivingDialog.org, and ToKnowWithCertainty.com.*

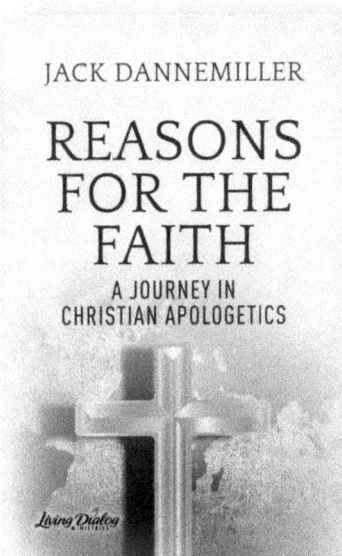

www.ingramcontent.com/pod-product-compliance
Lightning Source LLC
Chambersburg PA
CBHW060247030426
42335CB00014B/1620